U.S. ARMY GUIDE TO BOOBYTRAPS

U.S. ARMY GUIDE TO BOOBYTRAPS

DEPARTMENT OF THE U.S. ARMY

SKYHORSE PUBLISHING

Skyhorse Publishing books may be purchased in bulk at special discounts for sales promotion, corporate gifts, fund-raising, or educational purposes. Special editions can also be created to specifications. For details, contact the Special Sales Department, Skyhorse Publishing, 307 West 36th Street, 11th Floor, New York, NY 10018 or info@skyhorsepublishing.com.

Skyhorse® and Skyhorse Publishing® are registered trademarks of Skyhorse Publishing, Inc.®, a Delaware corporation.

Visit our website at www.skyhorsepublishing.com.

20 19 18 17 16 15 14

Library of Congress Cataloging-in-Publication Data

U.S. Army guide to boobytraps / by Dept. of the U.S. Army.
    p. cm.
  ISBN 978-1-60239-940-2
  1. Booby traps--Handbooks, manuals, etc. I. United States. Dept. of the Army. II. Title: US Army guide to boobytraps. III. Title: United States Army guide to boobytraps.
  UF860.U19 2010
  623.4'514--dc22

                                        2009039634

Printed in China

C. PULL-FRICTION

PULLING THE CHEMICAL
PELLET THROUGH THE
CHEMICAL COMPOUND
CAUSES FLASH THAT FIRES.
THE DETONATOR.

CHEMICAL
COMPOUND

CHEMICAL
PELLET

PULL-FRICTION FUZE, WEST
WW II GERMANY

D. PRESSURE-FRICTION

PRESSURE ON TOP OF THE
STRIKER FORCES ITS
CONE-SHAPED END INTO
THE PHOSPHORUS AND
GLASS MIXTURE IN THE
MATING SLEEVE, CAUSING
A FLASH THAT FIRES THE
DETONATOR

STRIKER

MATING SLEEVE

PHOSPHORUS
COMPOUND

MODEL 1952
FRANCE

7

E. CHEMICAL

(1) PRESSURE

PRESSURE ON THE TOP
BREAKS THE VIAL, FREEING
THE SULPHURIC ACID TO MIX
WITH THE FLASH POWDER,
PRODUCING A FLAME THAT
FIRES THE DETONATOR.

GLASS VIAL

SOFT ALUMINUM CASE

COTTON

WHITE FLASH POWDER

WW II GERMANY
BUCK CHEMICAL
FUZE

(2) DELAY

CRUSHING THE AMPULE RELEASES
THE CHEMICAL TO CORRODE
THE RETAINING WIRE, FREEING
THE STRIKER TO FIRE THE
DETONATOR. THE DELAY IS
DETERMINED BY THE TIME
NEEDED FOR THE CHEMICAL
TO CORRODE THE RETAINING
WIRE.

GLASS AMPULE
OF
CORROSIVE
CHEMICAL

RETAINING
WIRE
SPRING

M1 DELAY

8

*FM 5-31

FIELD MANUAL }
No. 5-31 }

HEADQUARTERS
DEPARTMENT OF THE ARMY
WASHINGTON, D.C., *14 September 1965*

BOOBYTRAPS

*This manual supersedes FM 5-31, 31 January 1956, including C 1, 16 December 1957, and C 2, 28 August 1959.

TAGO 5722-B—September

CHAPTER 1

CHARACTERISTICS OF BOOBYTRAPS

Section I. INTRODUCTION

1. Purpose and Scope

  a. This manual contains procedures, techniques, and expedients for the instruction of the soldier in the assembly, use, detection, and removal of boobytraps in combat.

  b. Included are descriptions and discussions of the design and functioning characteristics of standard demolition items — firing devices, explosives, and accessories — and missiles, such as hand grenades, mortar ammunition, artillery ammunition, and bombs.

  c. This manual also contains information on a variety of items and indigenous materials useful for improvising firing devices, explosives, and pyrotechnic mixtures for guerrilla warfare applications.

  d. Factory-produced boobytraps (dirty trick devices) are described. Most of these have been developed and used in the field by foreign armies.

  e. Safety measures pertinent to boobytrapping operations are provided for the protection of troops from casualty.

  f. The contents of this manual are applicable to nuclear and non-nuclear warfare.

2. Comments

Users of this manual are encouraged to forward comments or recommendations for changes for improvement. Comments should be referenced to the page, paragraph, and line of text. The reason for each comment should be given to insure proper interpretation and evaluation. Forward all comments directly to the Commandant, U.S. Army Engineer School, Fort Belvoir, Virginia 22060.

Section II. PRINCIPLES OF OPERATION

3. Types of Boobytraps

A boobytrap is an explosive charge cunningly contrived to be fired by an unsuspecting person who disturbs an apparently harmless object or performs a presumably safe act. Two types are in use —improvised and manufactured. Improvised boobytraps are assembled from specially provided material or constructed from materials generally used for other purposes. Manfactured boobytraps are dirty trick devices made at a factory for issue to troops. They usually imitate some object or article that has souvenir appeal or that may be used by the target to advantage.

4. Assembling Boobytraps

A boobytrap consists of a main charge, firing device, standard base (not always used), and detonator. Another item, the universal destructor, is an adapter for installing a firing device assembly in a loaded projectile or bomb to make an improvised boobytrap. Also, firing device assemblies are often attached to the main charge by means of a length of detonating cord.

5. Boobytrap Firing Chain

THE FIRING CHAIN IS A SERIES OF INITIATIONS BEGINNING WITH A SMALL QUANTITY OF HIGHLY SENSITIVE EXPLOSIVE AND ENDING WITH A COMPARATIVELY LARGE QUANTITY OF INSENSITIVE EXPLOSIVE.

RELEASED STRIKER FIRES PERCUSSION CAP

PERCUSSION CAP SETS OFF DETONATOR — PRODUCES FLAME

DETONATOR (BLASTING CAP) SETS OFF BOOSTER — PRODUCES SMALL CONCUSSION

BOOSTER DETONATES MAIN CHARGE (NOT ALWAYS USED) — PRODUCES LARGER CONCUSSION

MAIN CHARGE PRODUCES

EXPLOSION

6. Initiating Actions

THE INITIATING ACTION STARTS THE SERIES OF EXPLOSIONS IN THE BOOBYTRAP FIRING CHAIN.

A. PRESSURE

WEIGHT OF FOOT STARTS EXPLOSIVE ACTION.

B. PULL

LIFTING THE SOUVENIR STARTS EXPLOSIVE ACTION.

C. PRESSURE-RELEASE

MOVING THE STONE STARTS EXPLOSIVE ACTION.

MIAI PRESSURE FIRING DEVICE

M1 PULL FIRING DEVICE

TNT

M5 PRESSURE-RELEASE FIRING DEVICE

D. TENSION-RELEASE

RAISING LOWER SASH STARTS EXPLOSIVE ACTION.

DETONATING CORD

TNT

M3 TENSION-RELEASE FIRING DEVICE

TAUT WIRE

7. Firing Device Internal Actions

A FIRING DEVICE, WHEN ACTUATED MAY FUNCTION INTERNALLY IN MANY WAYS TO INITIATE THE FIRING CHAIN.

A. ELECTRIC

REMOVAL OF WEDGE BETWEEN CONTACTS CLOSES CIRCUIT AND FIRES ELECTRIC CAP.

THROUGH ELECTRIC CAP TO BATTERY

WOODEN WEDGE

TO ANCHOR

METAL CONTACTS

TO BATTERY

B. MECHANICAL

RELEASED STRIKER, DRIVEN BY ITS SPRING, FIRES PERCUSSION CAP.

M1A1

CHAPTER 2

USE OF BOOBYTRAPS

Section I. BASIC DOCTRINE

8. Tactical Principles

Boobytraps supplement minefields by increasing their obstacle value. They add to the confusion of the enemy, inflict casualties, destroy material, and lower morale. Boobytraps are usually laid by specialists. All military personnel, however, are trained in handli explosives and other boobytrapping material, so that they may, iɴ necessary, boobytrap a mine or install a simple boobytrap.

9. Authority

a. Army commanders issue special instructions for the use of boobytraps within their command. Supplies are authorized and provided as required to meet boobytrapping needs.

b. Army and higher commanders may delegate authority to lay boobytraps to as low as division commanders. All higher commanders, however, may revoke this authority for a definite or indefinite period, as the tactical situation may require.

c. Records of all boobytraps laid are prepared and forwarded to higher headquarters.

d. Enemy boobytraped areas, as soon as discovered, are reported to higher headquarters to keep all interested troops advised of enemy activities. If possible, all boobytraps are neutralized; otherwise they are properly marked by warning signs.

Section II. PLANNING

10. Tactical Effects

a. The ingenious use of local resources and standard items is important in making effective boobytraps. They must be simple in construction, readily disguised, and deadly. They may produce unexpected results if conceived in sly cunning and built in various forms. Boobytraps cause uncertainty and suspicion in the mind of the enemy. They may surprise him, frustrate his plans, and inspire in his soldiers a fear of the unknown.

b. In withdrawal, boobytraps may be used in much the same way as nuisance mines. Buildings and other forms of shelter, roads, paths, diversions around obstacles, road blocks, bridges, fords, and similar areas are suitable locations for concealing boobytraps.

c. In defense, boobytraps, placed in the path of the enemy at strategic locations in sufficient numbers, may impede his progress, prevent detailed reconnoissance, and delay disarming and removal of minefields.

11. Basic Principles

Certain basic principles, as old as warfare itself, must be followed to get the optimum benefit from boobytraps. Knowledge of these principles will aid the soldier, not only in placing boobytraps expertly, but in detecting and avoiding those of the enemy.

A. APPEARANCES
CONCEALMENT IS MANDATORY TO SUCCESS. ALL
LITTER AND OTHER EVIDENCES
OF BOOBYTRAPING MUST BE REMOVED.

BOOBYTRAP
CONCEALED IN BOOK

OBVIOUS PULLWIRE

B. FIRING
AN OBVIOUS FIRING
ASSEMBLY MAY DISTRACT
ATTENTION FROM A CUNNINGLY-
HIDDEN ONE.

C. LIKELY AREAS
DEFILES OR OTHER CONSTRICTED
AREAS ARE EXCELLENT LOCATIONS.

ANTIPERSONNEL
MINES

BOOBYTRAPPED
BOULDERS

BOOBYTRAPPED
BODY & RIFLE

BOOBYTRAPPED
ANTITANK MINES

D. OBSTACLES
ROAD BLOCKS, FALLEN
TREES, LITTER, ETC.,
ARE IDEAL LOCATIONS

PRESSURE-
RELEASE
FIRING
DEVICE

E. GATHERING PLACES
IN BUILDINGS, AT BUILDING ENTRANCES,
AND IN SIMILAR PLACES WHERE
SOLDIERS MAY MOVE OR
GATHER, DELAY CHARGES PAY OFF.

F. APPEAL TO CURIOSITY
BOOBYTRAPS LAID IN
BOLD POSITIONS TO DARE
THE CURIOUS GET RESULTS.

G. BLUFF
DUMMY BOOBYTRAPS, CONSISTENTLY
REPEATED, MAY ENCOURAGE CARELESSNESS.
AN OBVIOUS BOOBYTRAP MAY MASK
ANOTHER AND PERHAPS A MORE
DEADLY ONE.

EMPTY
EXPLOSIVE
CARTON

H. LURES
BOOBYTRAPS MAY BE BAITED. THE
UNEXPECTED DETONATION OF A DELAY
ACTION INCENDIARY OR EXPLOSIVE
BOOBYTRAP MAY SCATTER TROOPS OR
DETOUR THEM INTO A MORE HEAVILY LAID
AREA.

12. Location of Charges

a. Preparation. Small compact boobytraps are the most desire-able for use in raids in enemy-held territory. Each member of a team must carry his own supplies and be able to operate independently. Boobytraps should be assembled, except for the attachment of the firing device, before entering enemy territory. This will reduce the work at the site to the minimum.

b. Location. Charges should be placed where they will do the most damage. A charge detonated against a stone wall will expend its force in magnified intensity away from the wall. The force of an explosion on the ground will affect the surrounding air more if the charge is placed on a hard surface. This deflects the explosive wave upward. A charge detonating 6 to 10 feet above the ground will damage a larger area than one laid on or below the surface.

c. Characteristics. Many inexpensive boobytraps, simple to make and easy to lay, will delay and confuse the enemy more than a small number of the expensive and complex kind. Complex mechanisms cost more, require more care in laying, and offer little more advantage than the simple type.

13. Reconnaissance

Complete reconnaissance of an area is essential to good planning. Without this and the preparation of a program, boobytraps may not be used effectively. Boobytrap teams are best suited to survey a combat area to determine its boobytrapping possibilities.

14. Plan of Operation

a. The commander with authority to use boobytraps coordinates his plans with other tactical plans. Timing of boobytrap operations with movement plans is extremely essential. Boobytraps should not be laid in areas where friendly troops will remain for any appreciable length of time. Plans will indicate what is to be done, where and when it will be done, and the troops to be used. Generally, trained troops are assigned such tasks.

b. The plan authorizes the use of boobytraps and the types and densities required in specified areas, depending on the terrain, time, personnel, and material available. The completion of the detailed plan is delegated to the commander responsible for installation. Materials are obtained from unit supply stocks on the basis of the proposed action.

c. Complete coordination between the troop commander and the officer supervising boobytrap activities is essential. The area should be evacuated immediately following the completion of the job.

d. The commander installing boobytraps prepares a detailed plan indicating the site and the location, number, type, and setting. He assigns boobytrap teams to specific areas and the laying of specified types. The plan covers arrangements for supplies and transportation and designates the location where all preliminary work on boobytraps will be done. Time tables are established to insure completion of the work to comply with withdrawal phases of tactical plans.

e. In hasty withdrawal, when there is no time for planning, each team will be given a supply of material with instructions for making the best possible use of it in the time allowed.

f. Boobytrap planning must give proper consideration to all known characteristics of the enemy. Members of teams should study the personal habits of enemy soldiers, constantly devising new methods to surprise them. Repetitions may soon become a pattern easily detected by an alert enemy.

g. Withdrawal operations are the most desirable of all for laying boobytraps. When an enemy meets a boobytrap at the first obstacle, his progress throughout the area will be delayed even though no others have been laid. A few deadly boobytraps and many dummies, laid indiscriminately, can inspire great caution. Dummies, however, should be unserviceable or useless items. Never throw away material that may return to plague friendly forces!

Section III. INSTALLATION

15. Responsibilities

  a. A commander authorized to use boobytraps is responsible for all within his zone of command. He will keep adequate records showing their type, number, and location, and prepare information on those laid and on practices followed by the enemy.

  b. Management of boobytrap services may be delegated to the engineer staff officer.

  c. Unit commanders must know the location of all boobytraps in their areas and keep all subordinates so advised. Subordinates are also responsible for reporting to higher headquarters all new information obtained on enemy boobytraps.

  d. Officers responsible for laying boobytraps prepare plans, supervise preliminary preparations, and direct their installation. They forward to proper authority a detailed report of their progress, advise all concerned when changes are made, and report to engineer intelligence units the discovery of any new enemy devices or low-cunning practices.

  e. Engineer and infantry units, with special training, have the responsibility of installing and neutralizing boobytraps. Since adequate numbers of trainees may not always be available, all troops are given familiarity instruction in boobytrapping.

16. Procedures

  Like all activities involving explosives, boobytrapping is dangerous only because of mistakes men make. Prescribed methods must be followed explicitly in the interest of personal safety and overall effectiveness.

  a. Before assemblying a boobytrap, all components should be inspected for serviceability. They must be complete and in working order. All safeties and triggering devices must be checked to insure proper action, and for rust or dents that might interfere with mechanical action.

  b. If a boobytrapping plan is not available, one must be prepared on arrival at the site, so that the material obtained will be required items only. A central control point should be established in each boobytrap area where supplies may be unloaded and from which directions may be given. In areas where many boobytraps are concentrated, safe passage routes from the control point to each location must be marked clearly. Lines or tape may be useful where vegetation is heavy. The control man is the key man.

  c. Several teams may operate from one control point. Each team (rarely more than two men) is assigned to a specific area and supplies are issued only as needed. Each detail commander must make certain that every man knows his job and is competent to do it. Teams will remain separated so that one may not suffer from the mistake of another. When a job is completed, all teams must report to control man before going elsewhere.

d. One person in each team is designated leader to direct all work. If possible, members of a team will avoid working close together when a boobytrap is assembled. One member should do all technical work and the other be a helper to carry supplies, provide assistance needed, and learn the skills needed.

e. Boobytraps laid during raids into enemy held territory should be small, simple, and easily installed. Each member of a party must carry the supplies he needs. The use of boobytraps under these conditions, when accurate records are impossible, may be a hazard to friendly troops if raids into the same area should become necessary.

f. Procedure for installing boobytraps is as follows:

(1) Select the site that will produce the optimum effect when the boobytrap is actuated.

(2) Lay the charge, then protect and conceal it.

(3) Anchor the boobytrap securely, with nails, wire, rope, or wedges, if necessary.

(4) Camouflage or conceal, if necessary.

(5) Teams arm boobytraps systematically, working toward a safe area.

(6) Leave the boobytrapped area clean. Carry away all items that might betray the work that has been done, such as loose dirt, empty boxes, tape, and broken vegetation. Obliterate footprints.

17. Reporting, Recording, and Marking

Boobytraps are reported and recorded for the information of tactical commanders and the protection of friendly troops from casualty. Boobytrap installations are reported and recorded as nuisance minefields, whether the area contains both boobytraps and mines or boobytraps alone.

a. Reports

(1) *Intent.* This is transmitted by the fastest means available consistent with signal security. It includes the location of the boobytrapped area selected, the number and type of mines to be laid (if antitank mines are boobytrapped), boobytraps to be laid, the estimated starting and completing time, and the tactical purpose. The report is initiated by the commander authorized to lay the field and forwarded to higher headquarters.

(2) *Initiation of Laying.* This report is transmitted by the fastest means available consistent with signal security. It contains the location and extent of the field, total number of mines and boobytraps to be laid, and estimated time of completion. The commander of the unit installing

the field sends the report to the commander that directed him to lay it.

   (3) *Completion.* The report of completion is transmitted by the fastest possible means. It contains the number and type of boobytraps laid, location and extent of the field or area and the time of completion. The report is forwarded to army level. When boobytraps are laid, either alone or with mines, the report of intent and the report of initiation of laying will include the estimated number of boobytraps to be placed and the report of completion, the number placed.

  b. Records. Boobytraps are recorded as nuisance mine fields on the standard mine field record form. It is filled in as follows:

  (1) The general locations are shown on the sketch, using the appropriate symbol. Boobytrapped areas or buildings are lettered serially, "A" being the nearest to the enemy.

  (2) The number, types, locations, and methods of operation of boobytraps are entered in the NOTES section of the form. If space is lacking, additional sheets may be attached. If the boobytrap cannot be adequately described in a few short sentences, a sketch of minimum details will be included.

  (3) The record is prepared simultaneously with the laying of the boobytrap and forwarded through channels to army level without delay. If a standard form is not available, the data required must be entered and submitted on an expedient form.

  (4) Nuisance mine fields containing both mines and boobytraps are recorded as prescribed in FM 20-32. When the specific locations of boobytraps and manufactured devices cannot be accurately recorded (scattered laying in open areas) their number and type are entered in the notes section of the form and identified by grid coordinates.

  c. Marking. Boobytraps are marked by special triangular signs painted red on both sides. On the side facing away from the danger area, a 3-inch diameter white disc, is centered in the triangle and the word BOOBYTRAPS is painted in white across the top in 1-inch letters. The STANAG or new sign is similar except for the 1-inch white stripe below the inscription. Signs may be made of metal, wood, plastic, or similar material. They are placed above ground, right-angled apex downwards, on wire fences, trees, or doors, windows, or other objects or by pushing the apex in the ground. These working signs are used by all troops to identify friendly boobytraps during the period preceding withdrawal from an area, or to warn friendly forces of the presence of active enemy boobytraps.

d. Abandonment. When abandoning a boobytrapped area to the enemy, all markers, wire, etc., are removed.

e. Signs. Signs are also used to mark enemy boobytraps or booby-trapped areas.

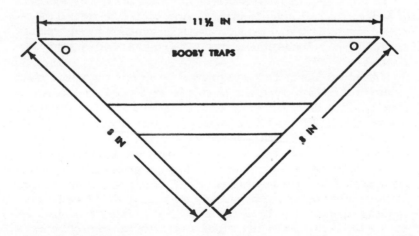

CHAPTER 3

BOOBYTRAPPING EQUIPMENT

Section I. FIRING DEVICES

18. Introduction

Many triggering devices are available for use in boobytraps. They include fuzes, igniters, and firing devices. All U.S. standard firing devices have the following advantages over improvisations; established supply, speed of installation, dependability of functioning, resistance to weather, and safety. All have a standard base coupling by which they may readily be attached to a variety of charges. For more detailed information see TM9-1375-200.

19. M1A1 Pressure Firing Device

    a. Characteristics.

| Case | Color | Dimensions | | Internal Action | Initiating Action |
		D	L		
Metal	OD	⅝ in	2¾ in	Spring-driven striker with keyhole slot release	20 lb pressure or more

Safeties	Accessories	Packaging
Safety clip and positive safety pin	3-pronged pressure head and extension rod	Five units with standard bases packed in cardboard carton. Thirty cartons shipped in wooden box.

    b. Functioning.

A pressure of 20 pounds or more on the pressure cap moves the trigger pin downward until the striker spindle passes through the keyhole slot. This releases the striker to fire the percussion cap.

PRONGED HEAD

LOCKING SAFETY

PRESSURE CAP

POSITIVE SAFETY

EXTENSION

FASTENERS

PROTECTIVE CAP REMOVED IN TRAINING AND BEFORE ATTACHING BLASTING CAP

STANDARD BASE

PROTECTIVE CAP   PERCUSSION CAP   STRIKER   SAFETY CLIP

KEYHOLE SLOT

c. Installing.

(1) Remove protective cap from base and crimp on a nonelectric blasting cap. *Crimper jaws should be placed no farther than ¼ inch from open end of blasting cap.*

(2) Assemble 3-pronged pressure head and extension rod and screw in top of pressure cap, if needed.

(3) Attach firing device assembly to standard base.

(4) Attach firing device assembly to charge.

TOP PRESSURE BOARD

NONELECTRIC BLASTING CAP

TNT

FRICTION TAPE

CRIMPERS

NOTE. If top pressure board is used, allow clearance space between it and top of prongs or pressure cap.

d. Arming. Remove safety clip first and *positive pin last.*

SAFETY CLIP

TNT

POSITIVE SAFETY

PRESSURE BOARD

20

e. Disarming.

    (1) Insert length of wire, nail, or original pin in positive safety pin hole.

    (2) Replace safety clip, if available.

    (3) Separate firing device and explosive block.

    (3) Unscrew standard base assembly from firing device.

20. M1 Pull Firing Device

  a. Characteristics.

		Dimensions			
Case	Color	D	L	Internal Action	Initiating Action
Metal	OD	9/16 in	3 5/16 in	Mechanical with split-head striker release	3 to 5 lb pull on trip wire

Safeties	Packaging
Locking and positive safety pins	Five units complete with standard base and two 80-ft spools of trip wire, are packed in chipboard container. Thirty chipboard containers are packed in wooden box.

b. Functioning.

A pull of 3 to 5 lb. on trip wire withdraws tapered end of release pin from split head of striker. This frees striker to fire the percussion cap.

c. Installing.

(1) Remove protective cap.
(2) With crimpers, attach blasting cap to standard base. *Crimper jaws should be placed no farther than ¼ in. from open end of blasting cap.*
(3) Attach firing device assembly to charge.

d. Arming.

    (1) Anchor trip wire and fasten other end to pull ring.

    (2) Remove locking safety pin first and *positive safety pin last.*

e. Disarming.

    (1) Insert nail, length of wire, or original safety pin in positive safety pin hole *first.*

    (2) Insert a similar pin in locking safety pin hole.

    (3) Cut trip wire.

    (4) Separate firing device and charge.

21. M3 Pull-Release Firing Device

a. Characteristics.

Case	Color	Dimensions D	L	Internal Action	Initiating Action
Metal	OD	9/16 in	4 in	Mechanical with spreading striker head release	Direct pull of 6 to 10 lb or release of tension

Safeties	Packaging
Locking and positive safety pins	Five units with two 80-ft spools of trip wire in carton, and 5 cartons packed in wooden box

b. *Functioning.*

(1) Pull.

A pull of 6 to 10 lb. on taut trip wire raises release pin until shoulder passes constriction in barrel. The striker jaws then spring open, releasing striker to fire percussion cap.

(2) Tension-release.

Release of tension (cutting of taut trip wire) permits spring-driven striker to move forward, separate from release and fire percussion cap.

c. *Installing.*

(1) Remove protective cap.

(2) With crimpers, attach blasting cap to standard base. *Crimper jaws should be placed no farther than ¼ in. from open end of blasting cap.*

(3) Attach firing device assembly to anchored charge (must be firm enough to withstand pull of at least 20 lb.).

(4) Secure one end of trip wire to anchor and place other end in hole in winch.

(5) With knurled knob draw up trip wire until locking safety pin is pulled into wide portion of safety pin hole.

d. Arming.

    (1) With cord, remove small cotter pin from locking safety pin and withdraw locking safety pin. If it does not pull out easily, adjust winch winding.

    (2) With cord, pull out positive safety pin. This should pull out easily. If not, disassemble and inspect.

e. Disarming.

    (1) Insert length of wire, nail, or cotter pin in positive safety pin hole.

    (2) Insert length of wire, nail, of safety pin in locking safety pin hole.

    (3) Check both ends and cut trip wire.

    (4) Separate firing device from charge.

Note. Insert positive safety pin first. Cut trip wire last.

25

22. M5 Pressure-Release Firing Device
a. *Characteristics*.

Case	Color	Dimensions			Internal Action	Initiating Action
		L	W	H,T		
Metal	OD	:1¾	15/16	11/16	Mechanical with hinged plate release	removal of restraining wt, 5 lb or more

Accessories	Safeties	Packaging
Pressure board	Safety pin and hole for Interceptor pin	Four firing devices complete and four plywood pressure boards in paper carton. Five cartons are packaged in fiber board box and 10 of these shipped in wooden box.

b. *Functioning*.
Lifting or removing retaining weight releases striker to fire the percussion cap.

c. Installing.

    (1) Insert a length of 10-gage wire in interceptor hole. Bend slightly to prevent dropping out.

    (2) Remove small cotter pin from safety pin.

    (3) Holding release plate down, replace safety pin with length of No. 18 wire. Bend wire slightly to prevent dropping out.

    (4) Remove protective cap from base and with crimpers, attach blasting cap. *Crimper jaws should be placed no farther than ¼ inch from open end of blasting cap.*

    (5) Secure firing device assembly in charge.

d. Arming.

    (1) Place restraining weight on top of firing device.

    (2) Remove thin wire from safety pin hole. If wire does not come out easily, restraining weight is either insufficient or improperly placed.

    (3) Remove heavy wire from interceptor hole. It should move freely. *Note. Withdraw thin wire first and heavy wire last. Follow arming procedure carefully*

e. Disarming.

    (1) Insert length of heavy gage wire in interceptor hole. Bend wire to prevent dropping out. *Proceed carefully, as the slightest disturbance of the restraining weight might initiate the firing device.*

    (2) Separate firing device from charge.

23. 15-Second Delay Detonator

a. Characteristics.

This device consists of a pull-friction fuse igniter, 15-second length of fuse, and blasting cap. The blasting cap is protected by a transit cap screwed on the base.

b. Functioning.

A strong pull on the pull ring draws the friction igniter through the flash compound, causing a flame which ignites the time fuse.

c. Installing.

    (1) Unscrew transit cap from base.

    (2) Secure device in charge.

d. Arming.

    (1) *Manual initiation.* Remove safety pin.

    (2) *Trip wire initiation.*

    (a) Attach one end of trip wire to anchor stake and the other to pull ring.

    (b) Remove safety pin.

e. Disarming.

    (1) Insert length of wire, nail, or original safety pin in safety pin hole.

    (2) Remove trip wire.

    (3) Separate firing device from charge.

24. 8-Second Delay Detonator

 a. *Characteristics.*

This device consists of a pull-type fuse lighter, 8-second length of fuse, and a blasting cap. The blasting cap is protected by a transit cap, screwed on the base.

 b. *Functioning.*

A strong pull on the T-shaped handle draws the friction igniter through the flash compound, causing a flame that ignites the time fuse.

 c. *Installing.*

   (1) Unscrew transit cap from base.
   (2) Secure device in charge.

 d. *Arming.*

   (1) Manual initiation: Remove safety pin.
   (2) Trip wire initiation.
   (a) Attach one end of trip wire to anchor stake and the other to pull ring.
   (b) Remove safety pin.

e. Disarming.
   (1) Insert length of wire, nail, or safety pin in safety pin hole.
   (2) Remove trip wire.
   (3) Separate firing device from charge.

25. M1 Delay Firing Device
a. Characteristics.

Case	Color	Dimensions D	Dimensions L	Internal Action	Delay
Copper and brass	Natural Metal	7/16 in	6¼ in	Mechanical with corrosive chemical release	4 min to 9 dos, identified by color of safety strip

Safety	Packaging
Colored strip inserted in hole above percussion cap.	10 units—2 red, 3 white, 3 green, 1 yellow, and 1 blue—and a time delay temperature chart packed in paper board carton, 10 cartons in fiber board box, and 5 boxes in wooden box.

b. Functioning.
   Squeezing copper half of case crushes ampule, releasing chemical to corrode restraining wire and release striker.

SAFETY STRIP

RESTRAINING WIRE

c. Installing.
  (1) Select device of proper delay.
  (2) Insert nail in inspection hole to make sure that firing pin has not been released.
  (3) Remove protective cap from base.
  (4) With crimpers, attach blasting cap to base. *Crimper jaws should be placed no farther than ¼ in. from open end of blasting cap.*
  (5) Secure firing device assembly in destructor and then in charge.

d. Arming.
  (1) Crush ampule by squeezing the copper portion of case.
  (2) Remove safety strip.

e. Disarming.
  There is no safe way of disarming this firing device. If disarming is necessary, insert an improvised safety pin through inspection holes.

26. M1 Pressure-Release Firing Device
  a. Characteristics.

Case	Color	Dimensions			Internal Action	Restraining Pressure
		L	W	Ht		
Metal	OD	3 in	2 in	2 in	Mechanical with springed latch release	3 lb or more

Safeties	Issue
Safety pin and hole for interceptor pin	Obsolete, but many are still available

b. Functioning.

Lifting or removing restraining weight unlatches lever, releasing striker to fire percussion cap.

c. Installing.

    (1) Insert a length of heavy gage wire in interceptor hole. Bend slightly to prevent dropping out.

    (2) Holding down latch, remove safety pin and replace with length of thin wire.

    (3) Remove protective cap from base and with crimpers attach nonelectric blasting cap. *Crimper jaws should be placed no farther than ¼ in. from open end of blasting cap.*

    (4) Assemble length of detonating cord, priming adapter, nonelectric blasting cap, and explosive block.

    (5) Attach free end of detonating cord to blasting cap on M1 release device with friction tape, allowing 6 in. of detonating cord to extend beyond joint.

d. Arming.

    (1) Place restraining weight on top of firing device.

    (2) Remove thin wire from safety pin hole. If it does not come out easily, restraining weight is either insufficient or improperly placed.

    (3) Remove heavy wire from interceptor hole.

Note. Proceed carefully.

e. Disarming.

    (1) *Proceed carefully as the slightest disturbance of restraining weight might unlatch lever and detonate the mine.* Insert length of heavy gage wire in interceptor hole. Bend wire to prevent dropping out.

    (2) Insert length of thin wire in safety pin hole, if possibile.

    (3) Separate firing device assembly and explosive charge.

Section II. DEMOLITION MATERIALS

27. Explosives and ·Accessories (For more detailed information, see FM5-25 and TM 9-1375-200.)

  a. TNT. This is issued in ¼, ½ and 1-pound blocks in a cardboard container with lacquered metal ends. One end has a threaded cap well. Half-pound blocks are obtained by cutting a 1-pound package in the center.

  b. M1 Chain Demolition Blocks (Tetrytol). This explosive consists of eight 2½-pound tetrytol blocks cast 8 inches apart onto a single line of detonating cord, which extends 2 feet beyond the end blocks. All blocks have a tetryl booster in each end. Each chain is packed in a have sack, and two haversacks in a wooden box.

  c. M2 Demolition Block (Tetrytol). The M2 demolition block is enclosed in an asphalt impregnated paper wrapper. It has a threaded cap well in each end. Eight blocks are packed in a haversack, and two haversacks in a wooden box.

d. M3 and M5 Demolition Blocks (Composition C3). These consist of a yellow, odorous, plastic explosive more powerful than TNT. The M3 block has a cardboard wrapper perforated around the middle for easy opening. The M5 block has a plastic container with a threaded cap well. Eight M3 or M5 blocks are packed in a haversack; and two haversacks, in a wooden box.

e. M5A1 Demolition Block (Composition C4). This is a white plastic explosive more powerful than TNT, but without the odor of C3. Each block is wrapped in plastic covering with a threaded cap well in each end. Twenty-four blocks are packed in a wooden box.

f. M112 Demolition Charge (Composition C4). This is composition C4 in a new package measuring 1 in. x 2 in. x 12 in. Each block has an adhesive compound on one face. Further information is not available.

g. M118 Demolition Charge. The M118 charge is composed of PETN and plasticizers. The detonating rate is approximately 23,000 ft. per second. Each package contains four sheets ¼ in. x 3 in. x 12 in. Each sheet has an adhesive compound on one face. Further information is unavailable.

h. Composition B. Composition B is a high explosive with a relative effectiveness higher than TNT, and more sensitive.

Because of its high dentonation rate and shattering power, it is used in certain bangalore torpedoes and in shaped charges.

i. *PETN.* This is used in detonating cord. It is one of the most powerful military explosives, almost equal to nitroglycerine and RDX. In detonating cord, PETN has a velocity rate of 21,000 feet per second.

j. *Amatol.* Amatol, a mixture of ammonium nitrate and TNT, has a relative effectiveness higher than that of TNT. Amatol (80/20) is used in the bangalore torpedo.

k. *RDX.* This is the base charge in the M6 and M7 electric and nonelectric blasting caps. It is highly sensitive, and has a shattering effect second only to nitroglycerine.

l. *Detonating Cord.*
(1) *Types I and II.* These consist of a flexible braided seamless cotton tube filled with PETN. On the outside is a layer of asphalt covered by a layer of rayon with a wax gum composition finish. Type II has the larger diameter and greater tensile strength.

WATERPROOFING

OUTER COVER

EXPLOSIVE

(2) *Type IV.* This is similar to types I and II, except for the special smooth plastic covering designed for vigorous use and rough weather.

m. Blasting Time Fuse. This consists of black powder tightly wrapped in layers of fabric and waterproofing materials. It may be any color, orange being the most common. As burning rate varies from about 30 to 45 seconds per foot, each roll must be tested before using by burning and timing a 1-foot length.

n. Safety Fuse M700. This fuse is a dark green cord with a plastic cover, either smooth or with single pointed abrasive bands around the outside at 1-foot or 18-inch intervals and double painted abrasive bands at 5-foot or 90-inch intervals. Although the burning rate is uniform (about 40 seconds per foot), it should be tested before using by burning and timing a 1-foot length.

o. ***M60 Fuse Lighter.***

   (1) ***To install:*** *Unscrew the fuse holder cap, remove shipping* plug, insert time fuse, and tighten cap.

   (2) *To reload:*

      (a) Insert primer base and primer in end of lighter housing.

      (b) Put washers and grommets in open end of fuse holder cap as shown, and screw fuse holder cap firmly on housing.

      (c) Unscrew fuse holder cap about three turns and insert a freshly cut end of time fuse into the hole in the cap until it rests against the primer.

      (d) Tighten cap.

(3) *To fire:*
 (a) Remove safety pin
 (b) Pull on pull ring.
 Note. Lighter is reusable after the insertion of a new primer and the reassembly of parts.

p. Electric Blasting Caps. Electric blasting caps have three lengths of leads—short (4 to 10 ft.), medium (12 to 14 ft), and long (50 to 100 ft). The short-circuit tab or shunt prevents accidental firing. It must be removed before the cap is connected in the firing circuit. Military blasting caps are required to insure detonation of military explosives.

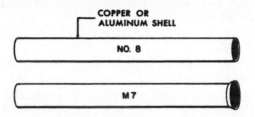

q. Nonelectric Blasting Caps. Two types are available, the No. 8 and the special M7, which resembles the No. 8 in appearance except for the expanded open end.

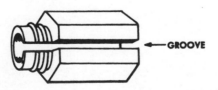

r. Priming Adapter. This is a plastic device with a threaded end for securing electric and nonelectric primers in the threaded cap wells of military explosives. A groove for easy insertion of the electric lead wires extends the full length of the adapter.

s. M10 Universal Destructor. The destructor is used to convert loaded projectiles, missiles, and bombs into improvised charges. The destructor has booster caps containing tetryl pellets. All standard firing devices with the standard base coupler screw into the top.

t. Antitank Mine Activator. This is a detonator designed for boobytrapping antitank mines. The top is threaded to receive all standard firing devices, and the base to screw in antitank mine activator wells.

PLUG

CORK GASKET

THREADS FOR STANDARD FIRING DEVICES

HIGH EXPLOSIVE CUP

28. Bangalore Torpedo

The bangalore torpedo is a group of 10 loading assemblies (steel tubes filled with high explosive) with nose sleeve and connecting sleeves. The loading assemblies may be used singly, in series, or in bundles. They are primed in four ways: by a standard firing device; a standard firing device, nonelectric blasting cap, length of detonating cord, priming adapter, and nonelectric blasting cap (para 29); a standard firing device, and length of detonating cord attached by the clove hitch and two extra turns around the cap well at either end of the loading assembly; and electrical methods (para 29).

29. M2A3 Shaped Charge

This charge consists of a conical top, conical liner, integral stand-off, threaded cap well, and 11½ pounds of explosive. It may be primed in three ways: by a standard firing device; a standard firing device, nonelectric blasting cap, length of detonating cord, priming adapter, and nonelectric blasting cap; and a priming adapter and electric blasting cap connected to power source.

30. M3 Shaped Charge

The M3 shaped charge is a metal container with a conical top, conical liner, threaded cap well, 30 pounds of explosive, and a metal tripod standoff. It may be primed in the same manner as the M2A3 shaped charge above.

METAL CONTAINER

THREADED CAP WELL

15 1/2"

15"

9"

31.   Introduction

Hand grenades, bombs, and mortar and artillery ammunition have wide application as improvised explosive charges. The only portion of these useful in boobytrapping, however, are the container and its explosive filler. The fuze is replaced by a standard firing device and an M10 universal destructor—an adapter designed especially for this purpose. The number and type of missiles useful in boobytrapping, however, are not limited to the examples given below.

32.   Hand Grenade

The M26 hand grenade, an improved model, consists of a thin metal body lined with a wire-wound fragmentation coil, fuze, and composition B explosive charge. It has a variety of applications to boobytrapping. The fuze is removed and a standard firing device is screwed directly into the fuze well or remotely connected by a length of detonating cord, priming adapter, and a nonelectric blasting cap.

33. 81MM Mortar Shell

This is converted by replacing the fuze with a standard firing device and a properly assembled destructor or by a firing device, length of detonating cord, priming adapter, nonelectric blasting cap, and a properly assembled destructor. If a destructor is not available the detonating cord and nonelectric blasting cap are packed firmly in the fuze well with C4 explosive.

34. High Explosive Shell

The high explosive shell is readily adapted to boobytrapping. The fuze is removed and replaced by a standard firing device and a properly-assembled destructor or a standard firing device, length of detonating cord, priming adapter, nonelectric blasting cap, and a properly-assembled destructor. If a destructor is not available, the detonating cord and nonelectric blasting cap are packed firmly in the fuze well with C4 explosive.

35. Bombs

These are adapted to boobytrapping in the same manner as high explosive and mortar shells. They are primed by replacing the fuze with a standard firing device and a properly-assembled destructor, or with a standard firing device, length of detonating cord, priming adapter, nonelectric blasting cap, and a properly-assembled destructor. If a destructor is not available, the detonating cord and blasting cap are packed firmly in the fuze well with C4 explosive.

36. Antitank Mines

A land mine may be used as the main charge in a boobytrap by removing the fuze and attaching a standard pull or pressure-release firing device in an auxiliary fuze well.

a. Pull.

    (1) Remove locking safety cotter pin in M1 pull firing device and replace with length of thin wire. Bend wire slightly to prevent dropping out.

    (2) Remove positive safety cotter pin and replace with length of thin wire. Bend wire slightly to prevent dropping out.

    (3) Remove plastic protective cap from standard base.

    (4) Assemble firing device, activator, and mine.

b. Pressure-Release.

    (1) Insert length of heavy wire in interceptor hole in M5 pressure-release firing device. Bend wire slightly to prevent dropping out.

    (2) Withdraw safety pin and replace with length of thin wire. Bend wire slightly to prevent dropping out.

    (3) Remove plastic protective cap from standard base.

    (4) Assemble firing device, activator, and mine.

    Note. The firing device must be set on a firm base. A piece of masonite is issued with the M5 for this purpose.

CHAPTER 4

CONSTRUCTION TECHNIQUES

Section I. Boobytrapping Mines in Minefields

37. Tactical Purpose

Antitank mines laid in mine fields are boobytrapped (or activated) primarily to make breaching and clearing as dangerous, difficult, and time consuming as possible in order to confuse, demoralize, and delay the enemy. Most standard U.S. antitank mines and many foreign antitank mines have auxiliary fuze wells for this purpose. See FM20-32 for more detailed information.

38. Methods

U.S. standard antitank mines are generally boobytrapped by means of a pull or a pressure-release firing device, or both, if desirable.

    a. Pull. Dig hole to proper depth to bury mine on firm foundation with top of pressure plate even with or slightly above ground level. Arm mine before boobytrapping.

(1) *Installing.*

    (a) Remove locking safety cotter pin and replace with length of thin wire. Bend wire slightly to prevent dropping out.

    (b) Remove positive safety cotter pin and replace with length of thin wire. Bend wire slightly to prevent dropping out.

    (c) Remove protective cap from standard base and assemble firing device, activator, and mine.

(2) *Arming.*

    (a) Anchor one end of trip wire to stake and fasten the other to pull ring.

    (b) *Remove locking safety wire first.*

    (c) Remove positive safety *last.*

    (d) Camouflage.

(3) *Disarming.*

    (a) Uncover mine carefully.

    (b) Locate boobytrap assembly.

    (c) Replace positive safety *first,* then locking safety.

    (d) Cut trip wire.

    (e) Turn arming dial of mine to *safe* and remove arming plug.

    (f) Remove fuse and replace safety clip.

    (g) Replace arming plug.

    (h) Recover mine and firing device.

b. Pressure-Release. Dig hole to proper depth to bury mine on firm foundation, with top of pressure plate even with or slightly above ground level.

(1) *Installing.*

(a) Insert length of heavy wire in interceptor hole. Bend wire slightly to prevent dropping out.

(b) Remove safety pin. Apply pressure on release plate until pin comes out easily.

(c) Insert length of light wire in safety pin hole and bend slightly to prevent dropping out.

(d) Remove protective cap from standard base and assemble firing device, activator, and mine.

(e) Place mine and firing assembly in hole, using pressure board to insure a solid foundation for firing device.

(2) *Arming.*

(a) Camouflage mine, leaving hole at side to remove safeties.

(b) Carefully remove thin safety wire *first*, then the interceptor wire.

(c) Complete camouflage.

(3) *Disarming.*
(a) Uncover mine carefully.
(b) Locate boobytrap assembly.
(c) Insert length of heavy wire in interceptor hole.
(d) Turn dial on pressure plate to "S" (safe) and replace safety fork.
(e) Recover mine and firing device assembly.
(f) Remove pressure plate, unscrew detonator, and replace shipping plug.
(g) Reassemble mine.

DETONATOR

SHIPPING PLUG

PRESSURE PLATE

SAFETY FORK

INTERCEPTOR HOLE

HEAVY WIRE

a. Antitank Mines.

The Communist European and Asiatic armies boobytrap mines in a much different fashion from that of the U.S. and other NATO countries. The Germans in World War II used both special antilift devices and antidisturbance fuzes, one of which has been copied by the French.

(1) Antilift devices.

(a) Russia

1. The Russians, Communist Chinese, and North Koreans boobytrapped wooden antitank mines by laying two of them, one on top of the other, in the same hole. The mines were connected by an MUV pull fuze and a pull wire, so that the bottom mine would detonate when the top mine was lifted.

2. The Russians in World War II also had a more sophisticated method—a special wooden antilift device, placed under the mine. This, however was readily located by probing. It consisted of an outer case, a charge, an MUV pull fuze, a pressure release lid supported on two coil springs, and a fuze access hole. Lifting the mine initiated the antilift. *This device is too dangerous to disarm.* Even though the pressure-release might be secured by a rope or length of wire, the chances of additional pull wires and boobytrap charges are too great to risk. Also deterioration of the wooden case from prolonged burial adds to the difficulty. *The best procedure is to blow all wooden antitank mines and antilifts in place.*

MUV PULL
FUZE

(b) *Czechoslovakia.* This satellite country has a wooden antitank mine (PT-Mi-D) that may prove extremely hazardous to breaching and clearing parties. Having an RO-1, pull fuze in each end, it is easily boobytrapped by means of wire anchored to a stake underneath the mine and extended through a hole in the bottom of the case to the fuze pull pin.

RO-1
PULL FUZE

PULL FUZE   PRESSURE BLOCK

PRESSURE PIECE   MINE LID   PRESSURE BOARD

COTTER PIN (BOTH ENDS OF MINE)

WOOD SHEAR DOWELS

STRIKER-RETAINING PIN

WOODEN LOCKING WEDGES

BOOSTER CHARGE (BLOCKS ALSO FILL SPACE IN MINE)   FUZE SUPPORT BLOCK

ACTIVATING PULL WIRE

STAKE

(c) *World War II Germany*. The German armies had several pressure-release devices for boobytrapping antitank mines. In a future war in Europe, these or facsimiles may appear on any battlefield.

    1 Nipolite all explosive antilift. This consisted of two oblong blocks of moulded explosive joined together with brass bolts and recessed to contain the metal striker assembly. It may be disarmed by inserting a safety in the lower safety pin hole.

SAFETY PINS

2 EZ. SM2 (EZ 44). This device consists of an explosive charge, a pressure-release firing mechanism, a safety bar and a metal case. When the safety bar is removed, the device arms itself by means of clockwork inside the case. *This device cannot be disarmed.*

SAFETY BAR

3 SF3. This antilift consists of an explosive charge, pressure-release striker assembly, safety bar, and chemical arming equipment. A turn of the safety bar crushes the glass vial, releasing the chemical to dissolve the safety pellet. *This device cannot be disarmed.*

SAFETY BAR

(2) **T. Mi. Z 43 and T. Mi Z 44** *antidisturbance fuzes.*

    (a) *Germany.* In addition to several antilift devices, the Germans developed two antidisturbance fuzes initiated by pressure or pressure-release for activating Teller mines 42 and 43. To arm, the fuze is placed in the fuze well and the pressure plate screwed down on top of the fuze, shearing the arming pin. Removal of the pressure plate initiates the pressure-release mechanism and detonates the mine. Although the T. Mi. Z 44 was an experimental model that never reached the field, copies of both fuzes are now in use in several European armies. *Mines armed with these fuzes can neither be identified by size, shape, marking, or color of the case, nor be disarmed.*

T Mi. Z. 43   T. Mi. Z 44

    (b) *France.* The French have a copy of the T. Mi. Z 43 antidisturbance (pressure and pressure-release) fuze, and Teller mine 43, named models 1952 and 1948 respectively. The fuze is placed in the fuze well and the pressure plate screwed down on top, shearing the arming pin. Removing the pressure plate actuates the pressure-release element, detonating the mine.

MODEL 1948
ANTITANK MINE

MODEL 1952
ANTIDISTURBANCE
FUZE

b. Antipersonnel Mines.

Antipersonnel mines are laid in antitank minefields to halt and delay enemy troops and make breaching and clearing as difficult, dangerous, and time consuming as possible. Enemy mine layers may increase this harrassment substantially by laying small blast type antipersonnel mines near the anchors and along the trip wires, which, according to procedure, must be traced from pull ring to anchor before cutting. These are extremely hazardous to breaching and clearing specialists who may detonate them unawares by the pressure of a hand, knee, or elbow on the pressure plate.

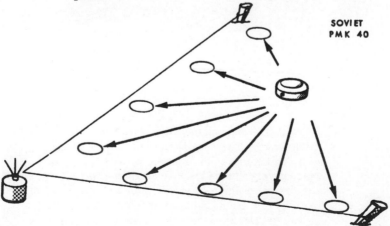

SOVIET
PMK 40

Section II. BOOBYTRAPPING BUILDINGS

40. Advantages

Boobytraps laid in buildings and their surroundings can be very effective. Buildings are very attractive to fighting men for they provide a degree of comfort and shelter from the elements. They are also useful for headquarters where plans may be made and communications carried on with greater dispatch.

41. Immediate Surroundings

a. Once a building has been occupied, it becomes the focal point for travel and communication from many directions. Thus the immediate vicinity becomes a potential location for boobytraps.

b. Dwellings in sparsely populated areas often have out buildings, wood piles, fruit trees, wells, fences with gates, walks, and other locations easily rigged to wound or destroy careless soldiers.

c. Delayed action charges detonated in buildings after they are occupied are extremely effective. Such charges, however, are difficult if not almost impossible to conceal, especially in large masonry and steel buildings, which may require a large quantity of explosive for serious damage or destruction. None but a most ingenious specialist, given time, help, and a wide selection of material can do this satisfactorily. In World War II, the Russians prepared such a boobytrap for the Germans. However, after long careful search, the charge and its clockwork fuze were located by means of a stethoscope. Small buildings, on the other hand, may be only moderately difficult to destroy by delayed charges.

42. Entrances

Curiosity prompts a soldier to investigate hurriedly an interesting building in his path. Women, loot, or mere inquisitiveness may be the motive. His rush to be the first inside makes all entrances excellent spots for boobytraps. For the foolish, a rigging connected to the front door, side door, or back doors may be sufficient. But for the experienced soldier, who may carefully seek entry to the basement first and then try to clear the building story by story, careful and ingenious effort may be required.

a. Basement Windows. Here boobytraps must be concealed to prevent detection by the enemy's breaking the pane or kicking out a door panel. Basement windows should be boobytrapped at the top or in the floor underneath.

b. Upper Floor Windows. Window charges are easier concealed in the weight box behind the jamb than in the wall or under the floor. Experienced hands can remove and replace window trim without obvious damage.

(1) *Nonelectric firing.*

    (a) Assemble M3 pull-release firing device, standard base, and blasting cap.

    (b) Place sheet explosive in weight box.

    (c) Bore hole in side jamb for pull wire.

    (d) Anchor one end of pull wire to window, and thread through hole in side jamb.

    (e) Attach free end of pull wire to ratchet on firing device.

    (f) Arm firing device.

    (g) Conceal boobytrap.

HOLE FOR PULL WIRE

M3 PULL-RELEASE FIRING DEVICE

2 1/2 LB SHEET EXPLOSIVE CHARGE

(2) *Electric firing.*

(a) Fasten two metal brackets to side of weight box close enough to wedge two flashlight batteries between.

(b) Place sheet explosive charge in weight box.

(c) Insert electric blasting cap in charge.

(*d*) Cut one leg wire and attach to lower bracket.

(e) Cut other leg wire to proper length to twist an uninsulated loop on end and fasten to hang in place just above top of window weight.

(f) On a length of leg wire twist on uninsulated loop around the leg wire hanging above the weight. Thread other end through other uninsulated loop and fasten to top clamp. Tape wire to window weight.

(g) Test circuit with galovonmeter first, then insert batteries between brackets.

(h) Conceal boobytrap.

c. Doors. Improved detection methods have made the use of boobytraps on doors, with charges, firing devices, and wires exposed, a waste of time and material, except for purposes of deception. The best location is the head or side jamb, not the sill, which is often recommended. The sill is exposed, so that one experienced clearing unit may easily locate the rigging while in the jamb, it is concealed by the doorstop.

    (1) *Head jamb rigging.*

        (a) Assemble M1 pull firing device, standard base, and non-electric blasting cap.

        (b) Assemble length of detonating cord, priming adapter, nonelectric blasting cap and explosive block.

        (c) Attach firing device firmly to stud and tape free end of length of detonating cord to nonelectric blasting cap.

        (d) Drill hole at proper place in header and head jamb.

        (e) Anchor one end of pull wire at proper place on door and thread free end through holes.

        (f) Close door and attach pull wire to pull ring.

        (g) Arm and conceal boobytrap.

(2) *Side jamb rigging.*

    (a) Attach metal brackets to side jamb close enough to wedge two flashlight batteries between.

    (b) Insert sheet explosive charge snugly between stud and jamb.

    (c) Place electric blasting cap in charge, and fasten one leg wire to top bracket.

    (d) Bore pull wire hole at proper spot inside jamb.

    (e) Cut other leg wire long enough to twist on an insulated loop on one end and fit over pull wire hole. Loop should be about ½ inch in diameter.

    (f) Twist on uninsulated loop on one end of leg wire and secure to lower bracket so that loop fits over pull wire hole. Fasten wire to jamb.

    (g) Anchor one end of insulated pull wire at proper spot on door, and thread free end through pull wire hole and loop fastened to jamb.

    (h) Close door. Fasten free end of pull wire to other loop to hold it snugly against stud.

    (i) Check circuit with galvonometer first, then

    (j) Install batteries between brackets.

    (k) Conceal boobytrap.

43. Structural Framework

a. In a building charges should be placed where detonation will seriously impair its structural strength, such as walls, chimneys, beams, and columns. Charges and firing devices must be carefully concealed to avoid detection.

b. In boobytrapping load-bearing walls, several charges should be laid to detonate simultaneously near the base. Chimneys and fireplaces are difficult to boobytrap for charges placed there are readily detected. These should detonate from intense heat.

c. Beams and columns when they collapse cause much more damage than walls because they bear much more weight.

    (1) In wooden beams, holes for concealed explosives should be bored close enough together for sympathetic detonation. An M1 delay firing device and detonator placed in a hole within the bulk explosive charge should suffice. Buildings of masonry and steel construction may also be booby-trapped with delay charges. The difficulty of the job depends often on the interior finish, type of decoration, heating ducts, air conditioning, and type of floors.

    (2) A column may be destroyed by a charge buried below ground level at its base. Although heavy delay charges like these are often considered mines, they are shown here because they may be found in boobytrap locations.

BULK
EXPLOSIVE

WOOD
PLUGS

M1 DELAY
FIRING
DEVICE

CONCRETE COLUMN

CONCRETE FLOOR

DELAY TYPE
FIRING DEVICE

CONCRETE
FOOTING

TNT BLOCKS

d. Loose floor boards sometimes are excellent objects for booby-trapping. The rigging must escape detection, however; otherwise, it will be ineffective. This rigging might be harder to detect if the support underneath is chiseled out to let the floorboard sink about ¼ inch when tramped on.

e. A double delay chain detonating boobytrap should be very effective if timed right and skillfully laid. *First,* is the explosive of a minor charge laid in an upper story damaging the building only slightly. *Then,* after a curious crowd has gathered, a second heavy charge or series of charges go off, seriously damaging or destroying the building and killing or wounding many onlookers.

Vacated buildings provide much opportunity for boobytrapping. Hurriedly departing occupants usually leave behind such odds and ends as desks, filing cases, cooking utensils, table items, rugs, lamps, and furniture. Electric light and power fixtures are also exploitable.

a. Desk. Because of its construction a desk is easily boobytrapped. If carefully placed the rigging may be nondetectable and if properly constructed, cannot be neutralized. Electric firing systems are the most suitable for this purpose. Sheet explosive is much better than other types, because its adhesive surface holds it firmly in place. Check the circuit with a galvonometer *before* installing the batteries.

b. Office Equipment. Many items used in offices have boobytrap potential.

    (1) *Telephone list finder.*
        (a) Remove contents from finder.
        (b) Assemble sheet explosive, shrapnel, and blasting cap.
        (c) Remove insulation from ends of wires and twist to form loop switch.
        (d) Place boobytrap in finder so that the raising of the lid draws the loops together.
        (e) Insulate inside of case from contact with loops with friction tape.

(f) Check circuit with galvanometer *first*, then install batteries.

Note. Batteries may be connected to legwires by wrapping them tightly in place with friction tape.

(2) *Card File.* A wooden card file can be boobytrapped effectively by the use of a mousetrap rigged as a trigger, a standard base with blasting cap attached, a support block fastened inside to hold the firing assembly at the proper level for operation, and a trigger block to hold the trigger in armed position.

   (a) Rig wire trigger of mousetrap with screw and metal strip.

   (b) Locate support block on strips at proper level to fix trigger in trigger block.

   (c) Bore hole in support block at proper place to admit standard base and blasting cap so that sheet metal screw will strike percussion cap.

   (d) Insert explosive, then support block with mousetrap, standard base, and blasting cap in position.

   (e) Raise trigger and close lid so that trigger is fixed in firing position.

TRIGGER BLOCK

MOUSE TRAP

STANDARD BASE

SUPPORT BLOCK 1/4" THICK

c. Electric Iron.
    (1) Remove bottom plate.
    (2) Insert bulk explosive and electric blasting cap.
    (3) Attach shortened leg wires to power inlet.

ELECTRIC BLASTING CAP

BOTTOM PLATE

BULK OR SHEET EXPLOSIVE

d. Teakettle.

    (1) Assemble sheet explosive, electric blasting cap and mercury element in teakettle.

    (2) Check circuit with galvanometer first, then install batteries.

Note. Batteries may be bound tightly in circuit with friction tape. For safety and ease of assembly, use a wrist watch delay in circuit (para 60*d*).

e. Pressure Cooker.

    (1) *Antidisturbance circuit.*

        (a) Assemble sheet explosive, mercury element, and electric blasting cap in cooker.

        (b) Check circuit with galvanometer *first*, then install batteries.

Note. Batteries may be bound tightly in circuit with friction tape. For safety and ease of assembly, use a wrist watch delay in circuit (para 60*d*).

SHEET EXPLOSIVE

MERCURY ELEMENT

ELECTRIC BLASTING

BATTERIES BOUND IN CONTACT WITH TAPE

FRICTION TAPE

(2) *Loop switch.*

    (1) Assemble sheet explosive and electric blasting cap.

    (2) Cut leg wires to proper length. Remove insulation from ends and twist to form loop switch.

    (3) *Check circuit with galvonometer.*

    (4) Fasten one leg wire (insulated) to lid to serve as pull wire.

    (5) Secure batteries in circuit by wrapping tightly with friction tape.

LOOP SWITCH

FRICTION TAPE

SHEET EXPLOSIVE

BATTERIES

f. Radio and Television Sets. Both sets may be boobytraped by assembling a charge and an electric blasting cap inside the case. The leg wires are connected in the circuit for detonation at turning of off-on switch.

Extreme care is required in connecting leg wires to prevent premature explosion.

ON-OFF SWITCH

OFF-ON SWITCH

g. Bed. Two methods may be used—a charge, nonelectric blasting cap, and pull firing device or a charge, batteries, electric blasting cap, and a mercury switch element.

    (1) *Nonelectric rigging.*

        (a) Assemble pull wire, M1 pull firing device, blasting cap, and sheet explosive charge.

        (b) Anchor pull wire so that a person sitting or lying on bed will initiate firing device.

        (c) Conceal boobytrap.

(2) *Electric rigging.*
   (a) Assemble sheet explosive charge, electric blasting cap, and mercury element.
   (b) Check circuit with galvanometer.
   (c) Place boobytrap on bed to initiate when its level position is disturbed.
   (d) Install batteries in circuit by wrapping tightly with friction tape.
   (e) Conceal boobytrap.

Note. For safety and ease of assembly, use a wrist watch delay in circuit (para 60*d*).

h. Chairs and Sofas. These may be boobytrapped nonelectrically and electrically as in *f* above. For nonelectric rigging the M1A1 pressure firing device, nonelectric blasting cap and sheet explosive charge are probably the most suitable. The sofa because of its size should have more than one rigging. If the electrical method is used *the circuit should be tested with the galvanometer before the batteries are installed.*

FIRING
DEVICE

i. Book. A book with an attractive cover is sure to invite examination.

    (1) Cut hole in book large enough to accommodate the rigging.

    (2) Assemble sheet explosive, electric blasting cap, mercury element, and shrapnel.

    (3) *Test circuit with galvanometer first,* then

    (4) Secure batteries in circuit by wrapping tightly with friction tape.

ELECTRIC
BLASTING CAP

MERCURY
ELEMENT

SHEET
EXPLOSIVE

NO. 9i2
BATTERIES

TAPE

SHRAPNEL

Section III. TERRAIN

45. Highways, Trails, and Paths

Boobytraps used along roads are a great help in slowing down
enemy traffic, especially if they are laid in and around other obstructions. Those placed on paths and trails are excellent against raid-
ing parties that must operate under cover of darkness.

46. Locations

Boobytraps in roadway obstructions should be concealed on the
enemy side. If the obstruction is heavy, requiring force to remove
it, boobytraps concealed underneath will increase its effectiveness.
Fragmentation charges are very destructive against personnel.
These include hand grenades; bounding antipersonnel mines with
their own special fuzes actuated by pressure or trip wire; ordinary
explosive charges covered with pieces of scrap metal, nails, gravel,
lengths of wire, nuts and bolts; and the like. The latter may be
actuated by any of the standard firing devices—by pressure,
pressure-release, pull-release, and pull.

    a. The jet of the M2A3 shaped charge from the roadside directed
into a moving vehicle is very destructive.

        (1) Assemble an M3 pull-release firing device and detonator,
length of detonating cord, priming adapter, and nonelectric blasting cap.

        (2) Drive anchor stake in berm at side of road and attach
pull wire. Drive stake or lay log, stone, or other object
on other side to support pull wire at proper height off
ground.

        (3) Attach firing device assembly to stake at proper position.

        (4) Fix shaped charge in position to direct explosive jet into
vehicle when front wheels hit trip wire.

(5) Attach free end of pull wire in hole in winch and draw taut.
(6) Screw priming adapter and nonelectric blasting cap in threaded cap well.
(7) Conceal boobytrap.
(8) Arm firing device.

Note: Cone may be filled with fragments.

ANCHOR STAKE

TAUT TRIP WIRE

M2A3 SHAPED CHARGE

PRIMING ADAPTER

NON-ELECTRIC BLASTING CAPS

DETONATING CORD TAPED HERE

M3 PULL-RELEASE FIRING DEVICE

b. An M3 shaped charge boobytrap placed overhead in a tree in a wooded area will destroy both tank and crew if located properly. Trip wire, being very thin and camoufloage-colored, is not easily detected by a driver.

(1) Assemble two firing devices (only one may be necessary) with detonators and lengths of detonating cord and a detonating cord primer.

(2) Attach firing assemblies and M3 shaped charge in position in tree, so that when the vehicle contacts the trip wires, the explosive jet will penetrate the crew compartment.

(3) Arm boobytrap.

c. Boobytraps laid in and along a narrow path may prove a delaying or frustrating obstacles to foot troops. These may be improvised shrapnel charges with a pressure-release firing device concealed under a stone, piece of wood, or other object, or with a pull or pull-release firing device and a trip wire. The latter would be very effective against patrols.

MOVEMENT

M5 PRESSURE-RELEASE
FIRING DEVICE

47. Special Locations

a. Abandoned serviceable or repairable items are frequently boobytrapped if time and equipment are available. Even unserviceable items may be rigged against scavangers who may search through the wreckage for useful things.

b. Abandoned ammunition should be exploited to the maximum. Chain detonations of connected mines or sections of bangalore torpedo are particularly effective.

c. Boobytraps are applicable to storage areas where materials cannot be removed or destroyed. Several charges strategically laid will prove very rewarding. A lumber pile provides excellent concealment for an explosive rigging. Sheet explosive may be used in many places where TNT is impractical, because of its size and shape. Here again chain detonations of explosive blocks and bangalore torpedos will do extensive damage, if the firing mechanism is properly located and cunningly concealed.

M3 PULL-RELEASE FIRING DEVICE

TNT BLOCKS

CONCEALED CHARGE

PRESSURE-RELEASE FIRING DEVICE

TNT BLOCKS

48. Abandoned Vehicles

a. *Truck Wheel.*

(1) Insert length of heavy wire in interceptor hole in firing device.

(2) Remove safety pin and replace with length of thin wire. Bend both wires slightly to prevent falling out.

(3) Assemble standard base, nonelectric blasting cap, and firing device.

(4) Assemble two 2-block explosive charges, nonelectric blasting caps, priming adapters, and length of detonating cord.

(5) In hole prepared under truck wheel, assemble bearing blocks (take weight off explosive charge), charges, bearing board, protective blocks (take weight off firing device), and firing device.

(6) Arm firing device.

(7) Cover boobytrap, and camoulflage.

FIRING DEVICE

TWO EXPLOSIVE BLOCKS ON EACH SIDE

TWO LENGTHS DETONATING CORD TAPED TO NONELECTRIC BLASTING CAP

b. Motor. The fan belt is an excellent anchor for a pull wire. The pull wire will be much harder to detect if anchored underneath the bottom pulley, from where it may be extended any length to the firing device and charge.

EXPLOSIVE CHARGE

TNT

DETONATING CORD TAPED TO NONELECTRIC BLASTING CAP

M1 PULL FIRING DEVICE

PULL WIRE

NONELECTRIC BLASTING CAP

PRIMING ADAPTER

CRIMPERS

M5 PULL-RELEASE FIRING DEVICE

TAUT WIRE

c. Electric System. A useful combination is a charge primed with an electric blasting cap with clamps attached to the leg wires. This may be attached to detonate by turning on the ignition switch, engaging the starter, braking, and the like.

d. Body. Another combination useful in rigging a seat or any other part of the vehicle body is a charge detonated electrically by means of a mercury switch element.

    (1) Assemble charge, electric blasting cap, and mercury element.

    (2) Place boobytrap in position and check circuit with a galvanometer.

    (3) Attach batteries in circuit by wrapping tightly with friction tape.

Note. Always check circuit before attaching batteries.

This rigging may be assembled in a small package for use in a seat cushion or separated for convenience for another location in the body of the vehicle.

CHAPTER 5

MISCELLANEOUS BOOBYTRAPS

Section I. STANDARD BOOBYTRAPS

49. Tactical Use

In World War II, every major power manufactured boobytraps to use against the enemy. Most of them were charged imitations of useful objects, which maimed or killed helpless soldiers that handled them. The defect common to all standard boobytraps however, is that after the first or second explosion, all others of the same type become ineffective. A "one-shot" job hardly justifies production costs.

50. Foreign Types

a. The Soviets used more standard boobytraps in World War II than any other combatant. A weird assortment of charged imitations of items issued to German soldiers were dropped from Soviet planes. Some of these were:

(1) Cartridge boxes, apparently filled with ammunition, containing high explosives and detonators.
(2) Bandage packets containing detonators and shrapnel.
(3) Bandage cases with Red Cross insignia rigged as mines.
(4) Rubber balls, about twice the size of a fist that detonated upon impact.
(5) Silver-grey light metal boxes or flasks that exploded when the lid was raised.
(6) Cognac bottles filled with incendiary liquid.
(7) Small red flags marked with an M and attached to mines that detonated when the flag was removed.
(8) Imitation earth-grey colored frogs that detonated when pressed on.
(9) Flashlights containing high explosive which detonated when the switch was moved.
(10) Mechanical pencils, watches, cigarette cases, cigarette lighters, salt cellars, and similar items that detonated when handled.

b. Knowing the German interest in books, the Soviets prepared a book boobytrap. The charge inside detonated when the cover was raised.

MAIN CHARGE

DETONATOR

BATTERY

WIRE LOOPS

PAGES CUT OUT TO RECEIVE
CHARGE AND FIRING DEVICES

c. The British also had a book boobytrap; but it was slightly more complicated than the Soviet version, above.

INSULATING WEDGE
FASTENED TO BACK OF SHELF

DEMOLITION BLOCK

ELECTRIC CAP

BATTERY

d. All sorts of dirty-trick devices were used by the enemy.
  (1) A flashlight was rigged with a charge and an electric detonator powered and actuated by the original dry cell battery switch, and circuit.

(2) Bottles designed to look like liquor bottles were filled with a liquid explosive detonated by a pull-friction fuze attached to the cork.

(3) A fountain pen, though very small, was rigged with an explosive charge, a spring driven striker to fire a percussion cap, and a detonator.

(4) The Japanese manufactured a pipe boobytrap with a charge, detonator, and spring-loaded striker.

(5) The Italians had a boobytrapped headset containing an electric detonator connected to the terminals on the back. The connection of the headset into the live communication line initiated detonation.

POWDERED EXPLOSIVE PACKED AROUND DETONATOR

DETONATOR

WIRE LEADS

DETONATOR WIRED TO TERMINALS AFTER THE DIAPHRAM IS REMOVED

(6) The Germans converted their own and enemy standard canteens into boobytraps. The explosive charge was detonated by a pull fuze and a pull wire connected to the cap. When partially filled with water and placed in its canvas case, it was very deceptive. The canteen boobytrap had an effective radius of 3 to 5 yards.

CANTEEN

PULL WIRE

WATER

PULL FUZE

MAIN CHARGE

DETONATOR

(7) Another German device was the boobytrap whistle. This consisted of a policeman's or referee's whistle with a charge and a metal ball covered with a layer of friction compound. Blowing the whistle moved the ball, igniting the friction compound and detonating the charge.

VIBRATING BALL
MADE OF
FRICTION MATERIAL

CHARGE

COMPOUND

(8) The German Peters candy bar boobytrap was ingenious indeed. The explosive charge, fuze, and thin canvas pull device were covered with chocolate.

CANVAS

51. Ingenuity

a. Through information on military operations in World War II, the U.S. soldier has been well-prepared for the dangerous mission of laying, detecting, and disarming boobytraps in conventional warfare. However, he now is virtually a novice in comparison with the cunning and ingenious present day guerrilla, who at the start was almost totally lacking in material and equipment.

b. Experience has shown that in guerrilla warfare, carried on by illy-equipped native populations, boobytrapping success depends largely on ingenuity. Explosive, a necessary element, is either improvised from commercial ingredients or captured from the enemy. Captured mines, ammunition, and other similar material are disassembled and every ounce of explosive saved.

52. Training

Every soldier should have some training in the lessons learned from the guerrillas, for many items they have improvised and the way they have used them are also applicable to conventional warfare. With little effort, a soldier may be trained so that with no military equipment whatever but with ample funds, he may prepare himself to fight effectively with materials available from merchants, junk piles, and salvage.

53. Application

The improvisations included in this section are gathered from numerous sources. Some may have wider application to boobytrapping than others. How the guerrilla may use them, however, is unpredictable. All are presented to stimulate initiative and arouse enthusiasm to out-do backward enemy peoples in devising and placing boobytraps and to develop a higher level of proficiency than ever before in their detection and removal.

54. Improvised Time Fuze and Explosive Caps

a. Fast burning fuse (40 inches per minute).

(1) Braid three lengths of cotton string together.

(2) Moisten fine black powder to form a paste. Rub paste into twisted string with fingers and allow to dry. If a powder is not available, mix 25 parts potassium nitrate (saltpeter) in an equal amount of water and add 3 parts pulverized charcoal and 2 parts pulverized sulphur to form a paste. Rub paste into twisted string and allow to dry.

(3) Check burning rate before using.

b. *Slow burning fuse (2 inches per minute)*.

(1) Wash three lengths of string or three shoelaces in hot soapy water and rinse.

(2) Dissolve 1 part potassium nitrate or potassium chlorate and 1 part granulated sugar in 2 parts hot water.

(3) Soak string or shoelaces in solution and braid three strands together. Allow to dry.

(4) Check burning rate.

(5) Before using, coat several inches of the end to be inserted into cap or material to be ignited with black powder paste (*a* (2) above).

c. *Electric Blasting Cap.*

(1) With file or other instrument make hole in end of light bulb.

(2) If jacket is not available, solder or securely fasten two wires to bulb—one on metal threads at side and other at metal contact on bottom.

(3) Fill bulb and empty portion of blasting cap with black powder. Tape blasting cap on top of bulb.

d. *Percussion Cap Assembly.*

    (1) Remove projectile, but not powder, from small arms cartridge.

    (2) Tape nonelectric blasting cap securely in cartridge.

NONELECTRIC
BLASTING CAP

SMALL ARMS
CARTRIDGE

FRICTION TAPE

55. Pull Firing Devices
a. *Tube and Striker.*

Assemble tube, spring, striker shaft with hole or with hex nut, soft wood or metal top plug, pull pin, and improvised percussion cap assembly.

Note. Always assemble firing device before attaching the improvised percussion cap assembly.

NONELECTRIC
BLASTING CAP

IMPROVISED
PERCUSSION
CAP

BLACK POWDER

b. *Clothes Pin.*

    (1) Wrap stripped ends of leg wires around clothes pin jaws to make electrical contact.

    (2) Assemble charge, adapter, electric blasting cap, and clothes pin.

    (3) Insert wooden wedge, anchor clothes pin, and install trip wire.

    (4) Check circuit with galvonometer *first*, then connect batteries.

c. *Stake or Pole Initiator.*

(1) Assemble stake or pole, container, metal contact plates, charge, electric blasting cap, and pull cord.

(2) Check circuit with galvonometer *first,* then connect batteries.

(3) Fasten down top of container and seal hole around stake with friction tape.

d. *Rope and Cylinder.*

(1) Cut leg wires to proper length.

(2) Prepare wooden end plugs and bore hole in one to receive leg wires.

(3) Thread leg wires through hole in block.

(4) Strip end of one leg wire and twist into loop, and secure other leg wire in position.

(5) Test circuit with galvonometer.

(6) Assemble metal cylinder, contact bolt, pull cord, charge, blasting cap, end blocks, and batteries.

e. *Trip Lever and Pull Pin.*

   (1) *Flat placement.*

        Assemble container, charge, improvised pull firing device
(*a* above) and trip lever.

   (2) *Sloping placement.*

        Assemble container, charge, improvised firing device
(*a* above) and stake.

STAKE

IMPROVISED
FIRING DEVICE

56. Pressure Firing Devices
a. *Mechanical Concussion.*

(1) Force striker into hole in pressure board.

(2) Insert wood or soft metal shear pin in shear pin hole.

(3) Assemble striker, metal tube, and improvised blasting cap (para 54).

METAL TUBE

STRIKER (NAIL)

COPPER
SHEAR PIN

IMPROVISED
BLASTING CAP

PRESSURE
BOARD

b. *Electrical.*

(1) *Lever arm.*

    (a) Attach contact blocks to ends of wooden levers.

    (b) Assemble wooden levers, rubber strip, and plastic sponge.

    (c) Attach leg wire contacts.

(2) *Flexible side.*

    (a) Attach metal contact plates to bearing boards.

    (b) Thread leg wires through holes in lower bearing board and attach to contact plates.

    (c) Attach flexible sides.

(8) *Springed pressure board.*

    (a) Assemble metal contacts, springs, bearing board, and pressure board.

    (b) Attach leg wires to metal contacts.

(4) *Wooden plunger.*

    (a) Assemble box, leaving one side open.

    (b) Assemble contact plate and three spacing blocks inside box.

    (c) Drill holes in spacing block for leg wires.

(d) Assemble plunger, metal release, contact block, metal contact, and contact screw.

(e) Thread leg wire through holes in spacing block and attach to contacts.

(5) *Metal box.*

(a) Attach metal contact to wooden contact block.

(b) Assemble contact block and metal contact, brackets, metal release, plunger, and wooden box lid.

(c) Bore hole in side of box for leg wires.

(d) Thread leg wires through hole in box.

(e) Attach one leg wire to plunger, the other to metal contact.

Note. Batteries may be placed inside box if necessary.

57. Tension-Release Firing Device

Attach stripped ends of circuit wires to ends of clothes pin to form contacts. Attach taut trip wires below contacts.

58. Pressure-Release

a. *Double Contact.*

   (1) Bore holes in top of mine body to accommodate long contacts.
   (2) Assemble pressure board, coil springs, wooden contact board and metal contacts.
   (3) Attach circuit wires.

CIRCUIT WIRES
MINE BODY
PRESSURE BOARD
SPRINGS
METAL CONTACTS

b. *Clothes Pin.*

   (1) Attach stripped ends of circuit wires to clothes pin to make contacts.
   (2) Place mine on top, keeping contacts apart.

STRIPPED ENDS
CIRCUIT WIRE
CIRCUIT WIRES

c. *Bottom Plunger.*

(1) Bore hole in bottom of mine case to admit plunger.

(2) Attach lower metal contact over hole.

(3) Assemble mine, pressure block, upper metal contact, and nonmetallic plunger.

(4) Attach circuit wires.

d. *Mousetrap.*

(1) *Mechanical*

See para 44 *b* (2)

(2) *Electrical*

(a) Remove triggering devices from mousetrap.

(b) Assemble trap, contact plate, and circuit wires.

(c) Place weight on top with striker in armed position.

59. Anti-Lift Devices

a. Loop Contact.

(1) Drill hole in bottom of mine to admit insulated pull wire.

(2) Assemble plunger, metal release, and contact plate.

(3) Attach circuit wires and bare loop to plunger contact and contact plate.

(4) Thread anchored insulated trip wire through holes in bottom of mine and contact plate and attach to bare loop.

b. Double Detonator.

(1) Drill three holes—one in bottom, one in partition, and one in side—to admit nonmetallic plunger and two electric blasting caps.

(2) Assemble blasting cap, leg wires, contact plates, plunger and pressure block.

(3) *Check circuit with galvonometer first.* Then connect batteries with friction tape.

(4) Install blasting cap connected to pressure firing device in side of mine.

103

c. *Sliding Contact.*
   (1) Assemble metal cap, nonmetallic tube or carton, sliding contact, wooden plug, and leg wires at contacts.
   (2) *Check circuit with a galvonometer first,* then connect batteries with friction tape.
   (3) Install assembly in tube.

60. **Delay Firing Devices**
   a. *Cigarette Timer.*
   (1) Test burning rate of time fuze and cigarette. (A cigarette usually burns at the rate of 1 inch in 7 to 8 minutes.)
   (2) Cut sloping end on length of time fuze.
   (3) Assemble sloped end of time fuze, match head, and cigarette.

   b. *Dried Seed Timer.*
   (1) Determine expansion rate of seeds.
   (2) Place in jar and add water.
   (3) Assemble jar, lid, circuit wires, metal contacts, and metal disk and secure with friction tape.

CIRCUIT WIRES

FRICTION
TAPE

BARED
ENDS

METAL DISK

DRIED BEANS, PEAS,
LENTILS OR OTHER
SEEDS

c. Alarm Clock Timers.
    (1) *Electric.*
        (a) Assemble base, metal contacts, and alarm clock.
        (b) Tie knot in one end of string. Thread other end
            through metal contacts and attach to alarm winding
            stem, which winches string and closes circuit.

Note. An alarm clock, being a very versatile delay, may be connected in many other ways.

CLOCK ATTACHED
TO BASE

SOFT METAL
CONTACTS

KNOT

STRING

CIRCUIT
WIRES

BASE

ALARM WINDING
STEM

(2) *Nonelectric.*

    (a) Drill hole in board of proper size to hold standard base tightly.

    (b) Remove standard safety pin from firing device and replace with easily removed pin.

    (c) Remove protective cap from standard base and crimp on nonelectric blasting cap.

    (d) Screw standard base with blasting cap into firing device.

    (e) Assemble alarm clock and firing device on board.

    (f) Attach one end of length of string to eye in safety pin and the other to alarm winding stem, which winches string and removes safety pin.

d. *Wrist Watch Timer.*

    (1) *One-hour delay or less.*

        (a) Drill small hole in plastic crystal and attach circuit wire with screw of proper length to contact minute hand.

        (b) Attach other circuit wire to case.

    (2) *Twelve-hour delay or less.*

        (a) Remove minute hand.

        (b) Drill small hole in plastic crystal and attach circuit wire with screw of proper length to contact hour hand.

        (c) Attach other circuit wire to case.

61. Bombs

a. Pipe Bombs.

   (1) *Grenade.*

      (a) Drill hole in cap or plug to admit length of time fuze.
      (b) Crimp nonelectric blasting cap to length of time fuze.
      (c) Assemble pipe, caps or plugs, time fuze primer, and explosive charge.

   (2) *Antidisturbance bomb.*

      (a) Drill hole in end cap to admit length of burnt time fuze to make a bomb look like a "dud."
      (b) Attach electric cap and mercury element on base.
      (c) Test circuit with galvonometer *first*, then connect batteries with friction tape.
      (d) Assemble bomb.

   Caution: If possible, assemble bomb *in place*, as the mercury element, when disturbed, may cause premature explosion. To assemble more safely and easily, attach wrist watch timer in circuit.

(3) *Shotgun bomb.*

    (a) Close one end of pipe with hammer, allowing opening for detonating cord primer or electric blasting cap.

    (b) Remove protective cap from M1A1 pressure or M1 pull firing device and crimp on nonelectric blasting cap.

    (c) Screw standard base with blasting cap into firing device.

    (d) Assemble pipe, shrapnel, wadding, explosive, nonelectric primer or electric blasting cap (for controlled firing), and proper firing device.

Note. The force of the explosive and the strength of the pipe are important in calculating the size of the charge.

b. Nail Grenade.

Attach nails to top and sides of charge by means of tape or string. Under certain conditions, nails may be required on only two sides, or even on one side.

c. Delay Bomb.

    (1) *Chemical delay.*

        (a) Crimp nonelectric blasting cap on base of appropriate M1 delay firing device.

        (b) Assemble firing device and charge in package.

        (c) Crush copper end of firing device with fingers.

        (d) Place package in suitcase or container.

Note. Use this bomb only when delay is necessary but accuracy is secondary, as the delay time of any chemical firing device varies considerably according to temperature.

NONELECTRIC
BLASTING CAP

CRIMPERS

(2) *Alarm clock delay.*
　(a) Drill hole in wooden base of proper size to hold standard base firmly.
　(b) Remove standard safety pin from M5 pressure-release firing device and replace with easily-removed pin.
　(c) Crimp nonelectric blasting cap on standard base and attach to firing device.
　(d) Assemble alarm clock and firing device on wooden base.
　(e) Attach one end of string in eye in pull pin and the other to the alarm winding stem so that its turning will winch the string and withdraw the pin.
　(f) Place assembly in suitcase or container.

CRIMPERS

M5 PRESSURE-RELEASE
FIRING DEVICE

STD
BASE

PROTECTIVE CAP

BASE

ALARM
CLOCK

NONELECTRIC
BLASTING
CAP

STRING

TAPE

STRING

PULL PIN

ALARM WINDING
SYSTEM

CHARGE

d. Envelope Bomb.

(1) Cut leg wires of electric blasting cap of proper length to make circuit.

(2) Strip insulation off ends of circuit wires and twist into ¼-inch loops to make loop switch.

(3) Test circuit with galvonometer *first*, then attach batteries.

(4) Assemble cardboard base, batteries, electric blasting cap, and explosive as package.

(5) Attach one end of string to loop switch so that it will pull the bared loops together to close circuit.

(6) Cut hole inside of envelope under flap.

(7) Fix package in envelope firmly and thread string through hole.

(8) Attach string firmly but concealed to underside of flap.

(9) Close envelope with elastic band.

ELASTIC BAND
(STRETCH AROUND ASSEMBLY)

WALLET TYPE ENVELOPE

CARDBOARD BASE

NO. 912 BATTERIES

ELECTRIC BLASTING CAP

SHEET EXPLOSIVE

STRING

LOOP
SWITCH

ATTACH STRING TO UNDERSIDE OF FLAP

e. *Hot Shrapnel Bomb.*
  (1) Remove protective cap from standard base and crimp on nonelectric blasting cap.
  (2) Screw base with cap in M1 pull firing device.
  (3) Crimp nonelectric blasting cap on one end of length of detonating cord, and install in Claymore mine.
  (4) Attach firing device to detonating cord with tape.
  (5) Assemble Claymore mine with priming and firing accessories and drum of napalm.
  (6) Arm firing device.

55 3AL DRUM NAPALM

CLAYMORE MINE

TAPE

TRIP WIRE

STD BASE

NONELECTRIC BLASTING CAP

MI PULL FIRING DEVICE

PROTECTIVE CAP

CRIMPERS

f. *Rice Paddy Bomb.*
  (1) Remove protective cap from standard base and crimp on nonelectric blasting cap.
  (2) Screw standard base with cap into M1 pull firing device.
  (3) Assemble firing device, detonating cord, priming adapter, nonelectric blasting cap, and explosive charge.
  (4) Attach charge to drum of napalm.
  (5) Arm firing device.

55 GAL DRUM NAPALM

DETONATING CORD

TAPE

EXPLOSIVE BLOCK

M1 PULL FIRING DEVICE

STD BASE

TRIP WIRE

PRIMING ADAPTER

OR MORTAR ROUND

PROTECTIVE CAP

NONELECTRIC BLASTING CAPS

CRIMPERS

PADDY FLOODED WITH HIGH OCTANE GASOLINE

WATER

DRUMS OF NAPALM SPACED INTERMITTENTLY

g. Tin Can Bomb.
   (1) Cut a notched metal contact disk to provide clearance for length of stiff insulated wire and $\frac{1}{8}$ to $\frac{1}{4}$ in. from walls of can.
   (2) Cut stiff insulated wire of proper length to support disk and strip insulation from both ends. Bend hook on one end to hold bare suspension wire.
   (3) Bend stiff wire to proper shape.
   (4) Assemble can, explosive, contact to can, blasting cap, insulated support wire, suspension wire and contact disk.
   (5) Check circuit with galvonometer *first*, then connect batteries.

62. Miscellaneous Charges

a. *Improvised Shaped Charge.*

(1) Cut strip of thin metal to make cone of 30° to 60° angle to fit snugly into container.

(2) Place cone in container.

(3) Pack explosive firmly in container to a level of 2x height.

(4) Attach standoffs to set charge above target at height of of cone.

2x diameter of cone.

(5) Attach blasting cap at rear dead center of charge.

b. *Improvised Antipersonnel Mine.*

(1) Assemble container, explosive, separator, and shrapnel. *Explosive must be packed to uniform density and thickness* (should be ¼ weight of shrapnel).

(2) Remove protective cap from standard base and crimp on nonelectric blasting cap.

(3) Screw standard base with blasting cap into proper firing device.

(4) Secure firing device in place.

(5) Fix primer in rear center of explosive and tape to firing device.

(6) Arm firing device.

CONTAINER
(METAL, PAPER, BAMBOO, ETC.)

SHRAPNEL

SEPARATOR
(CARDBOARD, COTTON WADDING, ETC.)

EXPLOSIVE

USE
MIAI PRESSURE

TAPE HERE

MI PULL

STD BASE

CRIMPERS

M3

PULL-RELEASE FIRING DEVICES

SHRAPNEL

DETONATING CORD PRIMER

EXPLOSIVE

c. *Platter Charge.*

(1) Assemble container, charge, and platter. Charge should weigh same as platter.

(2) Place primer in rear center of charge.

(3) Align center of platter with center of target mass.

(4) Attach and arm firing device.

115

CONTAINER (METAL, PAPER, BAMBOO, ETC.)

NONELECTRIC PRIMER

ELECTRIC BLASTING CAP

PLATTER

CHARGE

PLATTER (2-6 LB)

EXPLOSIVE

d. *Improvised Claymore.*

(1) Attach shrapnel to *convex* side of base and cover with cloth, tape, or screen retainer.
(2) Place layer of plastic explosive on *concave* side of base.
(3) Attach legs to *concave* side of base.
(4) Attach electric blasting cap at exact rear center.
(5) Attach firing device to firing wires at proper distance from mine for safety.

6"

10"

CONVEX BASE (TIN, METAL, CARDBOARD)

PLASTIC EXPLOSIVE 1/4 WT OF SHRAPNEL

RETAINER (CLOTH, SCREEN, WIRE, TAPE, ETC.)

ELECTRIC BLASTING CAP

LEGS

EXPLOSIVE AND SHRAPNEL

LEG WIRES

SHRAPNEL

FIRING WIRES

FIRING DEVICE

BASE

CHAPTER 6

BOOBYTRAP DETECTION AND REMOVAL

Section I. CLEARING METHODS

63. Technicians

a. Although engineer and infantry specialists are responsible for boobytrap detection and removal, all military organizations assigned to combat zone missions must provide trained men to assist them.

b. If possible, trained engineer, infantry, or explosive ordnance disposal units will search out and neutralize all boobytraps in front of friendly troops or prepare safe passage lanes. When discovered, boobytraps will either be disarmed immediately or marked by warning signs. Only the simple ones will be disarmed during attack. Those more complicated will be marked and reported for removal.

c. To avoid casualty, boobytrapped areas, especially villages and other inhabited places, should be bypassed, to be cleared by specialists later. Tactical units will neutralize boobytraps only when necessary for continued movement or operation.

64. Clearance Teams

Men who clear boobytraps are organized into disposal teams and assigned to specific areas according to their training and experience.

a. Direction and control is the responsibility of the person in charge of clearance activities, who will–

(1) Maintain a control point near at hand and remain in close contact with his clearance parties.

(2) Give assistance to disposal teams when required.

(3) Preserve new types of enemy equipment found for more careful examination by engineer intelligence teams.

b. Searching parties will be sufficient in number to cover an area promptly, without interfering with each other.

c. In clearing a building, one person will direct all searching parties assigned.

d. Open area clearance will be preceded by reconnaissance if the presence of boobytraps is suspected. Once boobytraps are found, search must be thorough.

e. Searching parties must be rested frequently. A tired man, or one whose attention is attracted elsewhere, is a danger to himself and others working with him.

65. Tools and Equipment

a. *Body Armor.* Armor of various kinds is available. Special boots and shoe pacs, also issued, will give greater protection against blast than boots generally worn.

b. Mine Detectors.

(1) Three mine detectors useful in the removal of boobytraps are issued: AN/PRS-3 (Polly Smith) and the transistorized, aural indication model, designed for metal detection, and AN/PRS-4 for nonmetallic detection. Of the metal detectors, the transistorized model is the lighter and more powerful. All three models have the same deficiences. They may signal a small piece of scrap as well as a metal-cased explosive or signal an air pocket in the soil, a root, or disturbed soil generally.

(2) Operating time should not exceed 20 minutes to avoid operator fatigue. *Tired operators often become careless operators.*

c. Grapnels. These are hooks attached to a length of stout cord or wire, long enough for the operator to pull a mine or boobytrap from place from a safe distance or from at least 50 meters behind cover.

d. Probes. Lengths of metal rod or stiff wire, or bayonets, are good probes for locating buried charges. Searching parties sometimes work with rolled-up sleeves better to feel trip wires and hidden objects.

e. Markers. Standard markers are carried by disposal teams to designate the location of known boobytraps, pending their removal.

f. Tape. Marking tape is useful for tracing safe routes and identifying dangerous areas.

g. Hand Tools. Small items, such as nails, cotter pins, pieces of wire, friction tape, safety pins, pliers, pocket knife, hand mirror, scissors, flashlight, and screw driver are very useful in booby-trap clearance.

66. Detection

a. The most careful observation is required for the detection of boobytraps. Soldiers must be trained and disciplined to be on guard, especially when moving over an area previously held by the enemy. Although a soldier may not be assigned the responsibility for their detection and clearance, he must be alert for any sign that may indicate their presence. He must also discipline himself to look carefully for concealed boobytraps before performing many acts of normal life.

b. Often prisoners of war through interrogation give information on new or unknown boobytrap devices that may aid in their identification and handling later on. Local inhabitants also often provide information on boobytraps laid in the neighborhood.

c. Searching for boobytraps and delayed charges is difficult and tedious, particularly when intelligence is lacking or inadequate. The extent of search required, the ease of placing and camouflaging, and the great number of devices available to the enemy make the clearance of all charges almost impossible. Searching parties, before being sent out, will be briefed on all that is known about enemy activities in the area.

67. Outdoor Searching Techniques

As boobytraps are so deadly and as a rule cunningly conceived and hidden, outdoor searching parties should be suspicious of -

a. All moveable and apparently valuable and useful property.

b. All disturbed ground and litter from explosive containers.

c. Marks intentionally left behind to attract or divert attention.

d. Evidence of former camouflage.

e. Abrupt changes or breaks in the continuity of any object, such as unnatural appearances of fences, paint, vegetation, and dust.

f. Unnecessary things like nails, wire, or cord that may be part of a boobytrap.

g. Unusual marks that may be an enemy warning of danger.

h. All obstructions, for they are ideal spots for boobytraps. Search carefully before lifting a stone, moving a low hanging limb, or pushing aside a broken-down wheelbarrow.

i. Queer imprints or marks on a road, which may lead a curious person to danger.

j. Abandoned vehicles, dugouts, wells, machinery, bridges, gullies, defiles, or abandoned stores. Also walk carefully in or around these as pressure-release devices are easily concealed under relatively small objects.

k. Areas in which boobytraps are not found immediately. Never assume without further investigation that entire areas are clear.

l. Obvious trip wires. The presence of one trip wire attached to an object does not mean that there are no others. Searching must be complete.

68. Indoor Searching Techniques

Those in charge of disposal teams should:

a. Assign no more than one man to a room in a building.

b. Indicate the finding of a large charge by a prearranged signal. All teams except those responsible for neutralizing large charges must then vacate the building immediately by the original route of entry.

c. Examine both sides of a door before touching a knob. Observe through a window or break open a panel. If doors and windows must be opened and both sides cannot be examined, use a long rope.

d. Move carefully in all buildings, for boobytraps may be rigged to loose boards, moveable bricks, carpets, raised boards or stair treads, window locks, or door knobs.

e. Never move furniture, pictures, or similar objects before checking them carefully for release devices or pull wires.

f. Never open any box, cupboard door, or drawer without careful checking. Sticky doors, drawers, or lids should be pulled with a long rope.

g. Not sit on any chair, sofa, or bed before careful examination.

h. Never connect broken wires or operate switches before checking the entire circuit. Such action may connect power to a charge.

i. Remove all switch plates and trace all wires that appear foreign to a circuit. Examine all appliances.

j. Investigate all repaired areas. Look for arming holes. Enlarge all wall and floor punctures. Cavities may be examined by reflecting a flashlight beam off a hand mirror. (This is also applicable for searching under antitank mines.)

k. Empty all fire boxes, remove the ashes, check fire wood, and move the coal pile.

l. Always work from the basement upward. Check, move, and mark everything movable including valves, taps, levers, controls, screens, and the like. A clockwork delay may not be heard if it is well hidden.

m. Double check basements and first floors—especially chimney flues, elevator and ventilator shafts, and insulated dead-air spaces. Check straight flues and shafts by observing from one end against a light held at the other. Dog-leg flues may be checked by lowering a brick from a safe distance.

n. Guard all buildings until they are occupied.

o. When possible and only after a thorough check, turn on all utilities from *outside* the building.

Note. A soldier by training can develop his sense of danger. Also by experience and careful continuous observation of his surroundings while in a combat area, he can develop an acute instinct that warns him of danger—a most valuable asset toward self-protection.

Section II. DISARMING METHODS

69. Neutralization

a. This is the making of a dangerous boobytrap safe to handle. If this is not possible, however, it must be destroyed. Neutralization involves two steps—*disarming* or replacing safeties in the firing assembly and *defuzing* or separating the firing assembly from the main charge and the detonator from the firing assembly.

b. Although types of boobytraps found in conventional warfare in a combat zone vary greatly, equipment used by most armies is basically similar except in construction details. Accordingly, a knowledge of the mechanical details and techniques in the use of standard U.S. boobytrapping equipment in conventional warfare prepares a soldier to some extent for dealing with that of the enemy. This, however is not true in guerrilla warfare. Most enemy boobytraps found recently in guerrilla infested areas, were cunningly and ingeniously improvised and laid. Such boobytraps can rarely be neutralized even by the most experienced specialists. These are discussed and illustrated in chapter 5.

c. Boobytraps may be neutralized by two methods. (1) Whenever the location permits, they may be destroyed by actuating the mechanism from a safe distance or detonating a charge near the main charge. These should be used at all times unless tactical conditions are unfavorable (2) When necessary, boobytraps may be disassembled by hand. As this is extremely dangerous, it should be undertaken only by experienced and extremely skillful specialists.

Note. Complete knowledge of the design of the boobytrap should be obtained before any neutralization is attempted.

d. In forward movements, all complicated mechanisms found are bypassed. These are marked and reported for neutralization later, when more deliberate action may be taken without harrassment by enemy fire.

e. All boobytraps exposed to blast from artillery fire or aerial bombing should be destroyed in place.

f. Boobytraps with unrecognizable or complicated firing arrangements should be marked and left for specialists to disarm.

(1) Electrically fired boobytraps are among the most dangerous of all. Though rare in the past, they now turn up frequently in guerrilla warfare. Some may be identified by the presence of electric lead wires, dry cells, or other batteries. Some are small containers with all elements placed inside which actuate at the slightest disturbance. These can hardly be disarmed even by experts.

(2) Another difficult type has delay fuzing—a spring-wound or electric clockwork for long delay periods or chemical action firing devices. As the time of detonation is uncertain, such boobytraps should be destroyed in place, if possible or tactically fesasible.

70. Rules of Conduct

a. Keep in constant practice by inspecting and studying all known boobytrap methods and mechanisms.

b. Develop patience. A careless act may destroy you and others as well.

c. Remember that knowledge inspires confidence.

d. Let only one man deal with a boobytrap. Keep all others out of danger.

e. If in doubt, get help from an expert.

f. Never group together when there is danger.

g. Be suspicious of every unusual object.

h. Regardless of nationality, consider every enemy a ruthless, cunning and ingenious killer.

71. Detailed Operations

a. *Destruction in Place.*

(1) If damage is acceptable, which is generally the case out of doors, the operator may initiate boobytrap riggings by their own mechanism or by a rope from a safe position (at least 50 meters away).

(2) The easiest method of getting rid of a boobytrap is to detonate a pound of high explosive adjacent to the main charge.

b. *Removal of Main Charge (Antitank Mine).*

Careful probing or search around the charge is necessary to locate and neutralize all antilift devices. Recognition of the type of firing mechanisms used is necessary to avoid casualty. All safety devices must be replaced. If complete neutralization seems doubtful, the charge should be pulled from place by a grapnel or rope from a safe location. After the charge is pulled, the operator should wait at least 30 seconds as a safeguard against a concealed delay action fuze.

c. *Hand Disarming.* None but trained specialists should undertake this job, unless the boobytrap's characteristics and disarming techniques are well known. Trained specialists only should inspect and destroy all unusual or complicated mechanisms for safety reasons and for information on new enemy devices. The following procedures for hand neutralization are for guidance only, as the exact sequence depends on the type of device and the manner of placement.

(1) Do not touch any part of a boobytrap before examining it thoroughly. Locate all firing devices and their triggering mechanisms.

(2) When tracing wires, look for concealed intermediate devices laid to impede searching. Do not disturb any wires during the examination of the boobytrap.

(3) Cut loose trip wires only after careful examination of all connecting objects and their functions and replacing all safeties.

(4) Trace taut wires and disarm all connected firing devices by replacing safeties. Taut wires should be cut only when the danger at both ends has been eliminated.

(5) Replace safeties in all mechanisms, using nails, lengths of of wire, cotter pins, and other objects.

(6) Never use force in disarming firing devices.

(7) Without disturbing the main charge, cut detonating cord or other leads between the disarmed firing devices and the main charge.

(8) Cut wires leading to an electric detonator—*one at a time.*

(9) When using a probe, push it gently into the ground. *Stop* when you touch any object. It may be a pressure cap or plate.

(10) Once separated, boobytrap components should be removed to a safe storage or disposal area.

d. *Special Precautions.*

(1) Be very cautious in handling delay mechanisms. Although there may be little danger before the appointed time, auxiliary firing devices may be present. All complicated and confusing devices should be destroyed in place or marked for treatment by specialists.

(2) Explosive containers of wood or cardboard, buried for long periods are dangerous to disturb. They are also extremely dangerous to probe if in an advanced state of decomposition. Deteriorated high explosives are very susceptible to detonation. Thus destruction in place of a boobytrap and in a concentrated area long exposed to moisture may detonate many others simultaneously.

(3) Metallic explosive containers, after prolonged burial, are often dangerous to remove. Oxidation may make them resistant to detection. After a time the explosive may become contaminated, increasing the danger in handling. Explosives containing picric acid are particularly dangerous as deterioration from contact with metal forms extremely sensitive salts readily detonated by handling.

(4) Fuzes of certain types become extremely sensitive to disturbance from exposure to wet soil. The only safe method of neutralizing or removing such deteriorated boobytraps is detonation in place.

72. Explosive Disposal

a. Usually, explosive items recovered by hand neutralization are destroyed by specially-trained explosive ordnance disposal units. Should untrained troops be required to do this, they should follow established procedures with great care. Explosives to be detonated should be buried in a pit at least 4 feet deep under 2 feet of earth, free of rocks or other matter that may become flying debris.

b. Components should be placed on their side or in position to expose their largest area to the force of the initiating explosive. Demolition blocks should be used for destruction of these components, if available; but bangalore torpedoes or dynamite may be substituted. Primed charges should always be connected to firing mechanisms by detonating cord, so that blasting caps may be connected at the last minute. This eliminates opening the pit in the event of a misfire. All persons engaged in disposal should take cover when explosive components are detonated. Despite the 2-foot layer of earth, fragments may be thrown at high velocity for several hundred yards.

APPENDIX I
REFERENCES

1. Field Manuals

FM 5–25   Explosives and Demolitions.
FM 20–32   Land Mine Warfare.

2. Technical Manuals

TM 5–280   Foreign Mine Warfare Equipment.
TM 9–1345–200   Land Mines.
TM 9–1375–200   Demolition Materials.

127

By Order of the Secretary of the Army:

HAROLD K. JOHNSON,
General, United States Army
Chief of Staff.

Official:

J. C. LAMBERT,
Major General, United States Army,
The Adjutant General.

Distribution:
Active Army:

DCSPER (2)	OS Maj Comd (5)
ACSI (2)	MDW (1)
DCSLOG (2)	Armies (5)
DCSOPS (2)	Corps (3)
ACSFOR (2)	Div (2)
CORC (2)	Div Arty (1)
CRD (1)	Engr Bde (2)
COA (1)	Engr Gp (2)
CINFO (1)	Engr Bn (2)
TIG (1)	Engr Co (2)
TJAG (1)	Engr Det (2)
CNGB (2)	USATC (2)
CofEngrs (2)	USMA (1)
USACDCEA (2)	Svc Colleges (2)
USCONARC (5)	Br Svc Sch (2)
USACDC (2)	PMS Sr Div Units (1)
ARADCOM (2)	USAECFB (2)
ARADCOM Rgn (1)	Instl (1)

NG: State AG (3); units—same as active Army.
USAR: Units—same as active Army except allowance is one copy to each unit.
For explanation of abbreviations used, see AR 320–50.

INDEX